ISBN 978-1-331-44327-8
PIBN 10190911

1 MONTH OF
FREE
READING

at

www.ForgottenBooks.com

By purchasing this book you are eligible for one month membership to ForgottenBooks.com, giving you unlimited access to our entire collection of over 700,000 titles via our web site and mobile apps.

To claim your free month visit:

www.forgottenbooks.com/free190911

Similar Books Are Available from
www.forgottenbooks.com

Andrew Robinson Bowes Esqr.

LIVES

OF

ANDREW ROBINSON BOWES, Esq.

AND THE

COUNTESS OF STRATHMORE,

WRITTEN FROM

THIRTY-THREE YEARS PROFESSIONAL ATTENDANCE,

FROM

LETTERS,

AND OTHER

WELL AUTHENTICATED DOCUMENTS.

BY JESSE FOOT, ESQ. SURGEON.

Quid verum atque decens, curo et rogo, et omnis in hoc sum.   HORACE.
Sine irâ et studio quorum causas procul habeo.   TACITUS.

London:
PRINTED FOR BECKET AND PORTER, 81, PALL MALL;
AND SHERWOOD, NEELY, AND JONES, PATERNOSTER ROW
By J. Bryan, Grocers' Hall Court, Poultry.

1812

CONTENTS.

CONTENTS.

LIVES, &c.

IT is natural to conceive that curiosity will be the greatest inducement for those who are solicitous to peruse the Lives of ANDREW ROBINSON BOWES, and the COUNTESS of STRATHMORE. They will expect to acquire a more extensive knowledge of transactions which have transiently passed in review before them, during a space of thirty-three years; they will naturally look for more information, more collected and digested than they have hitherto obtained; they will hope to be assisted in recalling to their recollection what has been but faintly registered, and to be furnished with new incidents and exact circumstances by which their floating and unsettled opinions may at length be more satisfactorily fixed; especially, since the scene is now for ever closed upon both of them ; since they and their contentions can no longer be heard, nor their separate artifices be henceforth debated before any earthly tribunal.

If this were the whole of my intention by publishing their LIVES, it might be a justification which could be maintained by reason ; but more use may be made of them, than curiosity merely, by the lesson which they will exhibit to all future generations. It will be seen that all adventitious appendages and decorative ornaments of fortune have not corrected their nature, enlarged their felicity, fortified their virtue, nor shielded their lives from the miseries consequent to vicious habits, unbounded passions, and lawless perpetrations. That neither scholastic discipline, the great mass of morality contained in the English library, the doctrine from the pulpit, nor the exhortation and example of honourable and anxious friends, could make the smallest impression upon their nature, or stem that career which was by each of them so libidinously pursued; a career almost unknown till now, in a country raised to the highest state of civilization, and where every advantage was at their command; where they, situated on the summit of fortune, could have beheld the fates not without commiseration of those whose vices were incurred by the positive force of narrow necessity. Neither of them received one single check from any compunctious visitings of nature; neither of them had disciplined their minds by the strict observance of any rule of right; both of them appeared as if they had been taken from a land not yet in a state of civilization, and dropped by accident where they have been found. Rather than that such extraordinary characters should be lost to society, I shall endeavour to rescue them from the gulph of oblivion, and to hold them up to the indignation and scorn of affrighted and insulted virtue.

Of A. R. Bowes I am about to speak first. By his Majesty's pleasure he assumed the name of Bowes instead of his native name, and as his original name is not seen in his signature, I have no right to disturb it; for if I did, I must expose his place of nativity, his family, and relatives, who I know are in possession of wealth, respectability, and honourable connexion. Two of his sisters I have seen, one of them for three months daily, and to whom I shall hereafter have occasion to refer particularly; and the other during the time her brother was upon his death bed. So that it must be apparent that I could give a very proper account of his genealogy, if I chose; but I am resolved to decline it, purely because I would not wish to stain their fair fame, by the insertion of their names in this disgraceful relation of one so closely allied by blood, but so estranged by nature. Their escutcheon, so far as I can prevent it, shall not be blotted by him. Nor shall I bring names into this relation which I can by any means keep out, as I know it was always not only possible, but desirable in Bowes to introduce himself to others upon false pretences. What he wanted of them, was never that he first spoke to them about The first introduction was merely to get a hearing from them, and by that to have the power, by the most artful and insidious means, to bend them and make them instrumental to his purposes.

I observe that Doctor Johnson, in his excellent Life of Savage, has given the freest scope to his sentiments on the conduct of the Countess of Macclesfield. His indignation seems to be raised to the highest degree, at the atrocity of her crimes, and therefore I shall not be wanting for a parallel, if I should, humbly as I must, tread in his steps, when similar aggravations present themselves, in the conduct of this Countess who is involved in this subject I am now upon. The two Countesses will admit of a very close comparison. The family of the Countess of Strathmore is already well known, and therefore if I say nothing more of her genealogy, yet nothing will be by my silence lost of information.

In the concealment of genealogy, I have also a precedent for suppressing Bowes's, in the Life of Psalmanazar, written by himself. As that Life perhaps has not been before every one who reads this, I will give some little explanation upon it.

Psalmanazar came to England and excited the general attention of men of fortune and letters, by the interesting relation he gave of himself. He said that he was a native of *Formosa,* and to prove it, he spoke and wrote the language of the Island, and gave a description of every thing relative to it. By certain occurrences, doubts were raised of his veracity ; his having once travelled out of the path of honour, put him to his shifts, and the frauds and impositions which afterwards marked his life, were at length by himself voluntarily confessed. It is to him that the public are indebted, for that learned article on the Jews, and the Hebrew language, now to be seen in Chambers's Dictionary.

Psalmanazar lived long enough to be struck with remorse; and to make atonement for all his forgeries and impositions, he begged pardon of all mankind; and what makes me think that he was sincere in his repentance is, that a consciousness of disgrace-

ful actions had not forsaken him; FOR HE NEVER
WOULD TELL THE REAL PLACE OF HIS BIRTH, NOR
DISCLOSE HIS PARENTAGE, THAT HE MIGHT NOT
LEAVE A STIGMA ON HIS COUNTRY AND HIS FAMILY.

In the year 1763 ANDREW ROBINSON BOWES was
a lieutenant in the 30th regiment. In that year the
regiment was disbanded, and ever since he has received the allowance of half pay. Supposing him to
have been then but twenty years of age, he would
have been now sixty seven ; but his sister says, he
was born in 1745, so that he could have been but
eighteen when he was put upon half pay. Be that as
it may.—Being quartered at Newcastle, he had the
address to marry Miss Newton, an heiress, with,
some say, £30,000, whilst he was yet but an ensign.

He was brought into the army by a relation, whom
I knew when he bore the rank of General. He resided in Berners Street, in 1777, was a most amiable
man, and I saw him at Bowes's levee, on the day of his
marriage with the Countess of Strathmore. Bowes
wanted to quit the army on his marriage with Miss
Newton, but his friend and relation then told him
the war would soon be over, and that half pay was
a thing easily received. Bowes took his advice.

The person of Bowes was rather in his favor, and
his address was, probably, when young, captivating.
His speech was soft, his height more than five feet
ten, his eyes were bright and small, he had a perfect command over them, his eye brows were low,
large and sandy, his hair light, and his complexion

A 3

muddy, his smile was agreeable, his wit ready, but
he was always the first to laugh at what he said,
which forced others to laugh also.   His conversation
was shallow, his education was bare, and his utter-
ance was in a low tone and lisping.   There was something uncommon in the connexion of his nose with
his upper lip ;   he never could talk without the nose
which was long and curved downwards, being also
moved ridiculously with the upper lip.   This I have
frequently laughed heartily at, when I observed the
ridiculous effect; it was seen much more when he
was in serious discourse, than in light conversation.
It was when he meant to be emphatic that it was
most discovered: in the light conversation he avoided
it, by not employing his upper lip beyond a certain
extent ; and in that case, he necessarily was forced
to lisp.

Bowes, after the year 1763, resided at Cold-Pig
Hill, the seat of Miss Newton's ancestors.   This
connexion brought him acquainted with families in
the vicinity.   He naturally would frequent assem-
blies and public meetings; and if what every body
says must be true, he in a violent fit of rage, tumbled
his wife down a whole flight of stairs, at one of those
meetings.   She bore the character of being a very
good woman, which in all probability increased her
sensibility, upon feeling her melancholy lot from the
choice she had made.   She soon took her departure
to another and better world.

Besides the vague report of Bowes's treatment
of his wife, as I have heard it, I have before

me two letters from residents of Newcastle. One of them says, that Bowes married Miss Newton, only child of William Newton, Esq. who was concerned in the coal trade, and with whom he got a large fortune; and treated her in a most cruel manner, so much so, that the impression left on people's minds on this subject is, that he shortened her days. The other comes to me in a letter from a mother now at Bath, to her daughter in London: it is as follows—

" What I can say about Bowes, I have left to the side of the sheet, that you may tear off, and give to Mr. Foot. Mr. Bowes, then Mr. S. came to Newcastle, with a marching regiment. He was ensign. I have seen him with his gorget on. He married Miss Newton, of Burnop Field, a lady I was acquainted with, and visited. She was not at all handsome; short, and very dark; but she had twenty thousand pounds, which, forty years ago, was reckoned a great fortune. Lady Bewick, and the late Mrs. Shafto, of Benwell, were believed to have forwarded the match. He made a very bad husband, and she was a most wretched wife, and brought no children alive into the world; which he much desired for his own sake. He made the bell of St. Nicholas toll for one that was dead born; but failed in proving it to be born with life. If he could have proved it, I understand the law gives a life-estate in the wife's property. He many times advertised the wood on the estates of Cold-Pig Hill, &c. to be sold, but the next week newspaper always produced a forbiddance from our friend Mr. Smith, Edward Jackson's father, and another person whose name I have forgot, who laid claim to the estate as next heirs. He behaved like a brute and a savage to his wife, and in a short time broke her heart. He knew secret ways of provoking her before company; and then if she looked displeased, or said any thing tart, he appealed to the company — HE TOOK PAINS to PLEASE HER, BUT COULD NOT.

"This passed for WORSE THAN NOTHING, to those who knew him. I do not know how it might be with those who were not acquainted with this accomplished villain. With his conduct after his marriage with Lady Strathmore, Mr. Foot will be well acquainted. I will write to Mrs. D. who knows many things of him, which I do not, and will be correct in the dates, &c. I will also write to Mrs. W. who, I am confident, knows many things also. But do not depend on me; write yourself to Mrs. D. She was at Bath, with Mrs. M. when Mr. Bowes thought proper to lampoon her, for coming into some public place in a hat. The lines were very severe

"I will put another strange anecdote of Bowes in the inside: — Bowes, upon some occasion, locked his wife in a closet, that would barely contain her, for three days, in her *chemise*, (some say without it,) and fed her with an egg a day. I have done a violence to my feelings, and wish what I have said may be of any use. Mrs. D. can tell a great deal more than me. Write without delay. Her name was Hannah Newton."

The character of Bowes being established by his treatment of this lady, not without just cause, it might be presumed, that it made the ladies shy of such a connexion. Therefore, nothing is reported of his having had the chance of another marriage for fortune, and no other sort of' marriage ever entered into his conception; he remained a widower, until the event took place between him and the Countess.

The interval of time between his first and second marriage, was filled up by the usual rotine of men of pleasure ; by gaming, cock-fighting, horse-racing, watering-places, and the petty-clubs in St. James's. Colonel S. well known at that time upon the turf, and at the gaming-table, was one of his chief companions. In all these amusements however artful he might and could play his part, nothing is heard to his disparagement, nor should I who knew him well, suspect it; for he was by nature a coward, and he felt the importance of not giving society an opportunity of finding it out. He possessed all the insinuation of that cast which will be found among men so happily pourtrayed in the character of IAGO.

Of t' COUNTESS of STRATHMORE I am now proceeding to give a short, but concise NARRATIVE.

The records of BIOGRAPHY are not confined to the virtuous alone, but embrace the general acts of human history, as they have passed in review, and as they are given for entertainment, improvement, and example to posterity. Good and bad cha-

racters are alike read in their turns; and instruction
of the highest value is to be found in all of them.
Their varieties adapt them to the genius, talent, and
disposition of all who seek to be amused and informed by this profitable study.

The most exalted talents of this last century have
been bestowed upon BIOGRAPHY, and the genius of
the late Doctor JOHNSON has been richly displayed
upon this theme. He never was at a loss for expression, and after having searched and discovered truth,
he was never found to hesitate in imparting it.
Hence it is seen, that in the Life of SAVAGE to which
I have already alluded, no one can read the mourn-
ful fate of SAVAGE without contemplating the conduct of the Countess of MACCLESFIELD.   Her
CONFESSIONS will remain as long as his Works, and
will be read even if the English should hereafter become a dead language ; and posterity will admire
with astonishment, the statement which this moral
author has so boldly given of the Countess, IN HER
LIFE TIME.

Of the CONFESSIONS of the Countess of STRATH-
MORE, I shall briefly observe, that I feel no disposition to awaken curiosity by laying them before
the public, because they were evidently extorted
from her, under the tyranny of BOWES. Not but
that they contain amoug many falsehoods some truths,
yet these are scattered and entangled with falsehoods, and when found and separated, like a few
grains among much chaff, are not worth the search.
The rest of the work, if it were true, is of that vile

and abominable nature, which will not admit of public inspection.

The Countess of Strathmore was a learned lady, and the house in Grosvenor Square might, for all I know, during the nine months of her widowhood, be fairly denominated a TEMPLE of FOLLY. The French have a celebrated Comedy upon learned ladies, called the *Bureau d'Esprit*, of which the Lady FOLLYCOURT is the patroness ; and I am very much mistaken if many Lady FOLLYCOURTS do not start up from the Institution in Albemarle Street. To see the vanity of preternatural excitements misapplied— to hear girls talk of being oxygenated and galvanized, must serve other thoughts besides science.

The mind of the Countess, by being bred up so much to flattery, by being always seen like a devotee at the shrine of admiration, was never left at liberty to be attentive to her most favoured delights, but was always solicited to embrace new objects, as if that mind was designed to comprehend the knowledge of all languages, and all the products of every country, in the four quarters of the globe. By setting her up as the patroness of the Arts, by her having designing people about her under these pretentions, and by her having had a husband who took no delight in them, she became a prey to that which well directed, might have saved her, and done honor to her and her family. Her talent was not in fault so much as the application of it. Her judgment was weak, her prudence almost none, and her prejudice unbounded. But there was intellect, of that sort

which required to be under the contruol of some
other.

To suppose that she, with a disposition to give an
audience with all her vast fortune, to every syco-
phant without either controul or enquiry, could escape from the snare she fell into, is to suppose that
flattery never yet undermined the heart, and that the
most designing strangers, the citizens of the world,
as they say of themselves, are the choicest body of
men to be called in, to regulate the felicity of domestic life, and even to mend the law, the custom
and morality of every establishment.

Now with all these learned pedants who depended
upon her, being opposed by any plain remonstrances
preferred before her, by any plain man of plain
meaning, what chance was there of her eventually
turning out otherwise, than as she will be seen, a
prey to the intrigue of the most savage, contempt-
able and low mind, that ever usurped over such
a possession.

But we are given to understand that learned ladies
exact a different scale for reasoning upon their actions,
than those of common life. The degree of excellence
in either, is dependent upon the notions of those
who sit in judgment upon their separate merits.
The Countess of Strathmore had learning, knew
a great many languages, and the study which was
the most valuable to her as a lady of fortune,
and to society, independent of the more immediate
and domestic accomplishments, was her great know-

ledge of botany. The Countess was the most intelligent female botanist of the age, and amongst all
her eccentricities of character which are to be seen
in her CONFESSIONS, and which tend to degrade her,
yet as she has there said nothing in her own praise,
being compelled by Bowes to destroy her own fame,
and to commit suicide upon her own character, I
may be allowed to state, that at this time, she was
finding creditable amusements during the day, by
building extensive hot-houses and conservatories at
Upper Chelsea. She had purchased a fine old man-
sion with extent of ground, well walled in, and
there she had brought exotics from the CAPE, and
was in a way of raising continually an increase
to her collection, when, by her fatal marriage, the
cruel spoiler came, and threw them like loathsome
weeds away.

I could from what I have collected also state,
in commiseration to the Countess's infirmities, that
the late Earl of Strathmore was not exactly calculated to make even a good learned woman a pleasing
husband. His Lordship's pursuits were always innocent and without the smallest guile, but they were not
those of science or any other splendid quality. A
sincere friend, a hearty Scotchman, and a good bottle
companion, were parts of his character. He would
rather suffer himself than sour the Countess by imposing any restraints upon her; hence were seen all the
learned domestics which haunted his house even in
his life-time.

Before Bowes obtained the Countess, he first of

all stormed the street door, and anti-chamber. There were with her, characters for the promotion of this, which she never engaged for such an undertaking. If the seed of discretion had been sown in her mind under a proper cultivation, the Countess might have been instead of infamy, a pattern of virtue. Lord BACON has said upon a young man who displayed in his character all the social virtues, that this young man must have had a good mother :—then perhaps as the Countess had a good father, a good mother, and a good husband, she was spoiled by over indulgence, ruined by over kindness, and corrupted by over caresses.

At the time that the late Earl of Strathmore went to Lisbon for the recovery of his health, I happened to be honoured with the strictest intimacy of a gentleman who owed all the patronage he enjoyed, to his Lordship's interest and friendship with the late Thomas Pitt, the first Lord Camelford, then his MA-JESTY'S COFFERER.

There was scarcely a day passed without my seeing this gentleman, and without my hearing at that time something or other of the history of the family and of the transactions in Grosvenor Square.

This gentleman resided in PALACE YARD, and although during his Lordship's residence in Town, and when he was in a state of good health, there was scarcely a week passed without paying his respects in Grosvenor Square, yet in his absence, he never was seen to shew any respect to the Countess.

The intelligence he received from a servant of the family yet remaining there, and yet faithful to the memory of his late master who died at LISBON, added to what he learned from Mr. and Mrs. O. and Lady A. S. gave him ample reason for withdrawing his attendance which was unwelcome to the feelings of friendship, and embittering to the memory of his dear and departed friend : for if there ever were a true friend upon earth, this gentleman was so to his patron the late Earl of Strathmore. He had a portrait of him constantly before his eyes, and the pride of heart was to be talking of his virtues.

The present Earl was then with his brother at a private school at NEASDEN, and I dare say has not forgotten the pleasure and gratification it gave him, when he saw this old friend of his father galloping on his GREY HORSE to the school door. Once if not twice I accompanied him, and I mean this merely to establish what I say.

From this gentleman I learned every circumstance about the state of the family; and such intelligence at such a point of time must be considered as valuable; as in my opinion, the conduct of the Countess of Strathmore which I am to enquire into, is limited to the small space of no more than nine months, from the time of the death of her Lord, in April, to her marriage with Bowes, in January.

This is the critical season for taking a view of the conduct of the Countess, and of the circumstances to which her conduct exposed her, as during these nine months from the death of the Earl of Strathmore, she was a free woman, unshackled and uncontrouled, and must be considered as responsible for all her deeds, and which whether what she committed during this interval be in the CONFESSIONS or not, she being compelled to make them; yet whatsoever in them refer to this period of her life and are true, must belong to the character of the Countess.

From the authority I have given, I am able to say that none of the relations and friends of the late Earl were acceptable in Grosvenor Square, during these nine months. That her Lord wrote her a letter from LISBON when all hopes of recovery were past, composed of admonition and forgiveness, and that the letter and account of his death were received with a cold and unfeeling indifference. That it was soon understood, that she had received the addresses of Mr. G—, a gentleman from India, who had served under Lord Clive in no very high capacity, but had made a fortune, and purchased land in Scotland; and every hour it was expected that the Countess was to be married to Mr. G—, that his visits were constant, and their airings open ; and that solemn promises had been made in the most solemn places, as a ratification of their intended union.

Besides, his Lordship having died so unexpectedly, and in the prime of life, the affairs of income were left perplexing, and some of his own estates in Scotland were obliged to be sold; and it was from serious reflection, that the late Lord's friends saw that a second marriage even with any body was against their, and the children's, interest.

Therefore, when the Countess was addressed by Mr. Gray, they kept aloof; and when she was abused and vilified, attacked and defended, in the Morning Print, during the months of November and December, previous to her marriage with Bowes in January, they, thinking that the abuse was useful to prevent the union of Gray with the Countess, suffered it to go on without the least opposition, rather pleased at the treatment she met, and for thus saying, I have the authority to tell, that the friend in Palace Yard and myself saw one of these attacks in manuscript before it was ever sent to the printer.

It was a letter condemning the Countess on her conduct towards her late Lord, and comparing her with the QUEEN in HAMLET, for being about to marry a second so soon after the death of her first husband; and this letter was written and published under the signature of HAMLET.

Now as there never has been an instance, I will take upon myself to say, neither before that time nor since, of such illiberal abuse against any person, and of any quality, and persevered in for such a length of time, how happened it, unless the friends of the late Earl had looked coldly on, that such an enormous outrage against decency could have been thus continued? Had they interfered, Bowes never might have been ultimately married

to the Countess; for all these contrivances, I am
now about to enumerate, sprung from his active,
mischievous, and too successful brain.   At this
stage of the statement, he was ANGUIS IN HERBA,
felt without being seen.   When the late Lord's
friends thought they were defeating the marriage
with Gray, by suffering this abuse to proceed
against the Countess in the Morning Print, they
actually laid the foundation of dispossessing GRAY,
and promoting BOWES.

Bowes's name at this time had scarcely been
heard of; I declare I had not then ever heard his
original name once mentioned by my friend of
Palace Yard.   I had heard of no other name, as a
lover, but Gray.

But all this while, the noise in the paper, and
the mischief, was Bowes's.   He had, as Sir Charles
Hanbury said of Mr. Hussey, who married a Countess also, an acquired knowledge of his way, knew
how to push his trade, and with what length to come
in at the heat he was contending for with the Countess against Mr. Gray.

Bowes was, in the first place, ten years younger
than Gray; in the second, more cunning; in the third,
bred up more regularly to the trade; in the fourth,
had the superior aid, the air, and the necessary
art of a man of the St. James's Coffee House.
There was no antiquated, dissipated, impudent,
and profligate nabob a match for him.

I really do conclude, without meaning the smal
lest reflection upon the friends of the late Earl of
Strathmore; that their fearful apprehensions of the
Countess's marrying Mr. Gray was the cause of
her falling, or rather plunging, into the arms of
Bowes, and I shall be able to prove this.

I shall now proceed to shew with what consummate art Bowes conducted this address, which
must be ever considered by his following, overtak-
ing, and passing Gray, who had the start of him
for the prize at least four months, a consummate
and successful masterpiece of art.

I will commence with what I believe may be
thought a deep scheme. Bowes knowing how
much the Countess hated all the friends of her late
Lord, in order to stimulate her to a second lover, if
ever she should determine to withdraw herself from
Gray, and which was his object, got a letter of
more than eight pages written, and sent it down to
Durham, that it might be delivered with the Durham post mark upon it. I have seen this letter,
with the Durham post mark upon it. This letter
was directed to the Countess, in Grosvenor Square,
and was to be supposed to be a copy of another
letter sent to Bowes, telling how an insulted,
abused, and deceived lady, to whom Bowes was
paying his addresses, and pledged, had sent to her
Ladyship this letter from mortification.

This letter was to inform the Countess how Bowes
had sacrificed her to the Countess; abused her

in the most severe terms, as one disappointed, af-
flicted, and forsaken; and denounced her vengeance upon him, and upon her, for faithless vows,
mercenary seductions, and fatal delusions.

But the strongest, deepest, and perhaps most
perfect plot that ever was designed was, that in
this letter, towards the latter end of it, the name
of Gray was introduced, and there one could easily
see all the spirit of the letter was intended.

It was purely this:---that the lady who wrote
this letter had at length found some consolation,
that her ladyship must be eventually married to
Mr. Gray, and that she then should once more be
happy; as by such an event her object would be
obtained, and her ladyship would be restored to
all her former family and friends, as Mr. Gray had
obtained several interviews with Mr. L-----n, Mr.
and Mrs. O-----d, and Lady A. S-----n, and all the
rest of her late Lord's friends and relatives, as he
had been to Paul's Walden, to her ladyship's mother, and as every thing was now most perfectly
adjusted, their mutual happiness was no longer
likely to be opposed to each other.

This was the very movement which eventually
defeated Mr. Gray. It gave the first imagination
of her intention to dispossess him of her favours.
That of his supposed connection with the late Lord
Strathmore's family, the artful letter pressing that
thought upon the Countess's prejudiced mind, made
her finally determine against Gray; and taking
into the account his age, his want of spirit, and his

languor, he soon became forbidden; she ceased to entertain him farther, and finally discarded him.

Besides the masked batteries which Bowes had erected, by the Strathmore family rejoicing at Gray's downfal, and by this cheating artifice practised upon the Countess through this copy of a letter, Bowes, never at rest till certain of success, was making his way into the house free and easy, not like Gray, but better. Every step he trod was an advanced piece of ground, which could not be contended against by any future rival. Comedy, which is not only the history, but the soul of life, shews the way to almost every necessary article which love may stand in need of: and there would have been a very moral reflection, if, in Grosvenor Square, a Countess, and one of the richest and wisest, could have been intruded upon by a lover, without his paving, by the favors of a lover, his way to the lady's room of audience.

The family now in the Square consisted of the Countess, Mrs. Parish, the governess of the chil dren, Miss Eliza Planta, sister to the governess, and confidant of the Countess, secretly in the in- terest of Bowes, the Rev. Mr. Stephens, just now about to be married to Miss Eliza Planta, also in the interest of Bowes; the chief visitors of the fa- mily were Mr. Magra, a botanist, and friend of Dr. Solander, and Mr. Matra, a consul at Barbary. These, besides accidental visitors, were the DRA- MATIS PERSONÆ, at the Temple of Folly, in Gros- venor Square.

Bowes had procured the good wishes of Miss Eliza Planta, and of the Reverend Chaplain, and of all the other domestics which might be necessary to his final success. Another stratagem he brought to his aid. Knowing that the Countess entertained romantic and visionary notions of things, he had a conjuror tutored to his wishes, and got Miss P. to make a party, with the Countess and some others, to have their fortunes told.

Bowes having thus far advanced in uninterrupted success, made up a match between the Chaplain and Miss Planta but a few days before his own with the Countess; and here I can avail myself of a corroborating proof, that no man can make advances so certain and successful as he who solicits his good fortune, by conferring good fortune upon others, and by assuming, in all ways, the acts of a generous gallant.

This Narrative having been carried on nearly to Christmas, and which was within three weeks of Bowes's marriage, the Countess had paid a visit to her mother, at PAUL's WALDEN, where she remained a few days; and whilst she was there, Bowes sent her the following letter:---

" Woman's a riddle. I never felt the proverb more than upon the honour of receiving your ladyship's letter. Eliza has, indeed, been playing within the curtain; had I been worthy to have had confidence in this business, I certainly should have advised a double plot. Your journey would have prevented any enquiry after the intention of your fair friend, and I then should have had the happiness of making my consort not only the conversation of the day, but the envy of the world. You draw a flattering picture of Mr. Stephens, was he any thing but Eliza's husband, I should not be pleased with his trait; but she deserves to be happy; and I hope he is every thing that she can wish. I always thought that Eliza had a good heart; but she has now convinced us that she has a great mind, above being trammelled by the opinion of guardians, relations, or pretended friends. A free choice is happiness; and bliss is the offspring of the mind. Those only possess joy who think they have it; and it signifies little whether we are happy by the forms our connections would prescribe to us or not. I believe it will not be denied, that many are miserable, under the opinion of the world, of their being very much the contrary. You tell me, that your good mother (Heaven bless her) is well employed for an old lady; but by the soul of ANGELICA* you vow, (and I know she was dear to you,) that her pursuits do not at this time engage your attention. Now by the living sick JACINTHA†, by every thing I have to hope, I swear, that I am highly interested in your present thoughts; and were I PROTEUS, I would instantly transform myself, to be happy that I was stroked and caressed, like them, by you; and, discovering the secret of your mind, I might experience what I hope Eliza will never be a stranger to, or be placed

beyond the reach of further hope. I am all impatience to see your Ladyship; I really cannot wait
till Saturday; I must have five minutes chat with
you before that time. You will think me whimsical;
but upon Thursday next, at one o'clock, I shall be
in the garden at PAUL'S WALDEN. There is a
leaden statue, or there was formerly, and near that
spot (for it lives in my remembrance) I shall wait;
and can I presume that you will condescend to
know the place? Eliza shall be our excuse for this
innocent frolic; and the civilities shall never be
erased from the remembrance of your faithful,
&c."

It is to be seen, that by this letter Eliza and
Bowes were upon the best of terms; that she was
the confidential friend of the Countess; that their
main object was to shake the mind of the Countess,
and to bring her to the resolution of discarding Mr.
Gray. And as if enough had not been already
done to secure this object, another letter from the
supposed injured lady was brought by the post
man, with the post mark of DURHAM upon it, to
Grosvenor Square, and ready for the inspection of
the Countess on her return from her visit to PAUL'S
WALDEN. This letter was not like the former, a
COPY of a letter to BOWES, but came in the shape
of one directly from the pretended lady to the
Countess. This letter was not written by Bowes,
but in all probability was framed by him.

" Pardon the liberty I took, of sending your
Ladyship the copy of the letter I wrote to Captain

S-----. The sacrifice I have made to this abominable man---the disobedience I have incurred from
the most indulgent parents---and the sport of my
friends, to whom I have imparted my confidential
prospects, drive me to despair. Besides, I love
him; and without him, though I am apprised of
his faithless nature, yet I am determined, at the
risk of my fortune, my character, my future comfort of life, and all that is dear to love and passion,
to throw myself into his arms. And must you,
who possess all the wealth of the North, think that
you have the right of thus defrauding an honest
heart, too fatally wounded and devoted, because,
not from your personal charms or intrinsic worth as
one of our unhappy sex, you thus lay claim to my
prize, but merely because you possess more acres,
and that you are a Countess. I will not, I cannot
sit silently down in submission to this usurpation;
I will haunt you night and day 'till I have procured
a restoration of that peace of mind, so long torn,
distracted, and broken down with wrongs, and
entirely through you, by this foul and dear se-
ducer.

Why don't you abide by your first love as I do?
Why should Mr. Gray be abandoned by you for
the sake of a man who stands before you a perjured
lover? Why am I to be the sacrifice to your al-
mighty influence, and thus plunged into despair
and oblivion, for no end but to gratify the wanton-
ness of your caprice? And that you, Madam, you
may have the pride and exultation of despoiling and
erecting upon my despair your felicity!

For the sake of whatever is dear to our sex—for the feelings which unhappy woman owes to one another, pray indulge me with your kind attention. One moment's pause in the prosecution of your present cruel resolution may save me from destruction, and make your character immortal. Cultivate Mr. Gray's affections, because your late Lord's friends and relations will accept of him as your husband, but not of Captain S-----. It is impossible that Mr. Gray should keep these secrets from you. Mr. Gray has had the address, (which my simple and easy fool never could obtain) of first establishing his pretensions to you, upon the confidence and zeal of your late Lord's relations and friends, Mr. L-----, Mr. and Mrs. O-----, and Lady A. S-----. It is with their warm approbation that he has wisely made his way to your heart. Plunge not, therefore, an artless, hopeless, desponding, and forsaken maiden as I am into destruction and utter ruin, but restore some ray of comfort to the unfortunate

S."

Having prosecuted this intrigue, (some would say conspiracy,) and brought the circumstances almost to a conclusion, by which the Countess was decoyed into the power of Bowes; and approaching to that period of the lives of those remarkable personages, when, in vindication of the Countess, Bowes had a RENCONTRE with the Editor of the Morning Print, the contents of which, in constant columns, displayed attacks upon her conduct and her virtue, I shall avail myself of the opportunity, before I go into a minute detail of this event, of closing with a description of the person and appearance of the Countess at this present moment of time, and before the iron rod of her tyrant had despoiled her of her charms, broken down her spirit, wasted her body, and eclipsed her faculties.

If I were to attempt hereafter to do what I am about to do now, like a picture of youth, the resemblance would be false, when compared with the original, after the changes which have been wrought by time, by cruelty, by sorrow, and despair.

Of the person of the Countess, when I first saw her, I shall, as far as I recollect, give a description. It was the morning after the duel, that she entered Bowes's apartment, at the St. James's Coffee House. The Countess at this time was scarcely thirty years of age: she possessed a very pleasing ENBONPOINT; her breast was uncommonly fine; her stature was rather under the middle class; her hair brown; her eyes light, small, and she was near sighted; her face was round; her neck and shoulders graceful; her lower jaw rather under-hanging, and which, whenever she was agitated, was moved very uncommonly, as if convulsively, from side to side; her fingers were small, and her hands were exceedingly delicate. She appeared in very fine health; her complexion was particularly clear; her dress displayed her person, it was elegant and loose; she glowed with all the warmth of a gay widow, about to be married; and she prompted all around to be certain that she was conscious of having obtained, with all this difficulty, that which, without this eclat, she never might have been thus blessed: she seemed poor silly soul! as if she blessed the duel, and blessed every body about it, for the sake of the precious prize the contest brought her. She blessed even the sword that was used by Bowes in the duel, took it home with her, and slept with it constantly at the head of her bed all the while she was in Grosvenor Square.

Having now nearly finished my narrative of the Countess of Strathmore, who is just about to surrender her liberty, and consequently her responsibility to all purposes, noble and ignoble, I shall close it with a copy of the promised letter, under the signature of HAMLET, which my friend of Palace Yard and myself first saw in manuscript, and which is here extracted from the Print, and is as follows.

To this worthy friend of Palace Yard I must first be permitted to bid my sincerest farewel, as a man capable of strong friendship, and whose regard for the family of the Earl of Strathmore did not cease with life, for he was, by his will, buried at PAUL'S WALDEN, in the chancel, and left £100. to the clergyman of the parish.

I will also give the answer of MONITUS to this letter of HAMLET, or otherwise it might be suspected that I have inserted the letter of HAMLET to feed the vanity of a young man, now become older; when the fact is, that I only introduced it to assert my knowledge of the case; whereas this letter of HAMLET; with the answer of MONITUS, will shew that the whole of the dispute was maintained radically from the family quarrel.

Morning Post, Friday, Jan. 3, 1777.

Mr. Editor,

The polite circulation of your paper, and the candor you display in admitting whatever may be said on both sides, when either politics, fashions, or characters, are the game in pursuit, make me not doubt but you will give insertion to this. I read lately a letter in your paper, which on account of the subject with which it is connected, has attracted my attention, and has induced me for once to step forward to inform MONITUS, and his noble client THE COUNTESS OF GROSVENOR SQUARE, that their menaces of fatal blows, or louring dangers, will not intimidate me from joining in the general cry, and entering my protest upon all occasions against a character, whose leading features are a proper object for the scorn and derision of the public.

No one wants to know whether the paragraph in the Morning Post originated from BLOOMSBURY SQUARE, or a TOMB AT EPHESUS. It would have been well for the house of S-----------e, had the noble dame procured only the slight satirical ill will of any of the family, that would have just kept a few gossips awake at a tea-table; and have slept at the first SANS PRENDRE.

MONITUS artfully parries, but does not vindicate; he is too flimsy to alter the opinion they have formed of his NOBLE MISTRESS, who knew her when HYMEN first graced her with a noble lord, a handsome, virtuous youth, who brought her honour, and sought her happiness; who knew her, when her fondness for him was fulsome to excess; who knew her, when sickness laid his heavy hand upon him, and can bear witness to her cold indifference to the letters that passed between them, where all was ceremony, and where there was not enough of prudence in her to supply the want of love. Who has not seen her since in the Mall gracing the hymenial throng? Had she not better been employed in her closet, MONITUS perusing the letters she received from her fond and doting noble lord? or in visiting her eldest son, whom she has forsaken?

HAMLET.

On Tuesday, January 7th, 1777, there is an answer to HAMLET, at a very considerable length from MONITUS, in the same paper.

THE COUNTESS OF STRATHMORE DEFENDED.

HAMLET, the gracious HAMLET, has at last met with the Ephesian Ghost, and defended by his minister of grace, he steps forward to inform

MONITUS and his mistress, that it was armed with the completest steel.

And always so completely armed are truly virtuous characters, that even the strongest oppression will not be able to withstand those convincing proofs of a generous hearted woman; who from a benevolent disposition of mind, has raised and supported a whole family of ungrateful wretches! indulged their vanity, increased their estate, and made them respectable; who in return for such favors now meanly and basely expose every little misconduct of her's in a public print; and in the language of SCORPIO SCURRILITAS, inhumanly threatens to harrow up her soul! But lest I should be thought to enter too freely upon a cause that so justly requires to be vindicated, I beg leave, through your candor, Mr. Editor, which I have experienced upon former occasions, to inform HAMLET, that I have no noble client nor the least interest in defending a character so grossly imposed upon ; but rather let him look back and consider MONITUS a youth much injured by their notice.

Deeply concerned for the conduct of the noble Countess, in those few trivial faults which are laid to her charge, and which did increase certainly the satirical ill-will of a few; yet I am more concerned when I observe a long chain of falsehoods propagated daily, with no other intent than to cause a general conflagration, and forcibly to wrest her from the good opinion of those that were neither acquainted with her benevolent, nor misguided

transactions; but who are now led to give credit
to gossip-hatched aspersions of those draining
wasps, who long extracted the substance of this
flower, which they had found to be pure, as well
as it was rich!

HAMLET with a becoming grace, offers a protest
against a character whose leading features are a
proper object of scorn and derision, but at the same
time declares he does not want to know from
whence originated those fulsome falsities, but will
join in the cry of the principal leader; yet afterwards asserts, he will not alter the opinion he has
formed against the noble COUNTESS; since HYMEN
first graced her with a noble Lord.

Such being the disposition of HAMLET, he must
be a prejudiced being, and therefore should submit
to a proper explanation of those elucidations,
equally mysterious as without foundation. "MON-
ITUS will not parry," but he will vindicate, and
shake off that flimsy art, which HAMLET has accu-
sed him of, and lead him forth from the mistaken
crowd! First, then let us behold a woman born to
the greatest possession of wealth, that can enrich
a single subject in all the British dominions:
educated in the paths of virtue and innocence, she
glides through the first stages of youth, untutored
in those arts and deceptions so familiar to courts.

She was the darling and hope of a fond parent,
and prudently made choice of a partner for life,
from whose mutual embraces sprung the present

pledges of their dearest loves. With an unalterable conduct of goodness and affection, she, tried every means to gain respect, not only from her lord, but from every one that beheld her. Happy must that man have been, when blest with a woman whose purity of mind led her to those acts of true benevolence and charity, which thousands of the poor can testify. When sickness laid his heavy hand upon her lord, she then beheld him dearer to her than at the first moment after their union! Where are they that bring proof either of her cold indifference, or that all was ceremony instead of affection! or that can bring witness of a want of prudence in her to supply the want of love! When to all that were around her, the agonizing and heart-felt sorrow was obvious, when she found her dearest lord was departing and at length no more.

Under such affliction, let us suppose the noble Countess left a widow, rich and respectable, among all ranks of people, open to receive the caresses, and all the honors due to a person of the highest rank of nobility, formed to enjoy such pleasures as would divert the melancholy gloom from her mind. She no sooner goes to the PLAY or walks in the PARK than there are a thousand eyes upon her, and every step to attract her attention! all striving to great favor, and every tongue employed how to become her favorite. For what? Because she abounds in wealth; and how charming and profitable would it be were it possible to prey upon her weakness, or delude her into those snares her sex are most subject to! Had the so much disappointed flight of BLOOMSBURY·JILTS, continued in the good graces of her their kind benefactress, it would have been' well for them; but let them be assured, that all their vollies of slander, and of every method that iniquity can prompt them to do, will never reinstate them in her beneficence or esteem, which retrieved them from that poverty, only known to their kind keeper.

MONITUS.

The continued provocations which appeared, particularly in one morning paper, and which was then read by the town more than any other, seemed at the approach of the time of the duel more aggravating, both in the attacks and defences of the Countess's conduct. She appeared to have been watched every where, and to have been brought out of her house in Grosvenor Square, on purpose that the public might know and see more about her, than could' have been obtained within it, without pointing to somebody there. She was dragged like a victim at a bull feast. There were also previous to the night of the duel, or rather rencontre, some sharp sparrings in the paper, as if the spirit of the Editor scorned to suppress an attack upon himself, when he from motives of candor inserted the attacks upon others. This was all highly proper. There was most certainly a storm expected, the horizon was dark and threatening, but the quarter was unknown from whence the element would open, and the tornado descend.

At the time when the scene of the rencontre was

drawing near, Bowes then resided at the St. James's Coffee house. He had come to town at this season of the year purely to carry his plan with the Countess into effect. His associations were all of that sort, which idle and uneducated men of pleasure pick up at the gaming houses, clubs, horse races, watering places, &c. In such a society, all are much upon a level in point of morals. They carry on a traffic amongst each other, exchange their horses, their dogs, and their mistresses, for the capricious accommodation of one another; and they keep a sharp look out for the opportunity of obtaining money, and improving their fortunes, from heir or heiress, by play or marriage, no matter which.

Bowes's connection in Durham, by his marriage with Miss Newton, afforded him a plea of introduction to the Countess's house. He had no occasion to say who he was, if he could once get in, and obtain an audience, in Grosvenor Square. By this time he had succeeded in the familiar enjoyment of his entré---had overcome all the obstacles, and was upon the same footing with Mr. Gray, or a stronger; but be was more restless and active than Gray, and never suffered one single engine in his employ to stand still as long as he remained unmarried to the Countess. He had made all the male literati his friends, and had secured the smiles of the female. The Countess's companion, Eliza, was propitious to him, and had tasted of his kindness. He made his attack upon the Countess by every stratagem that all men and women could devise.

Such was the situation of Bowes and the Countess on the evening of the RENCONTRE of which, after I have given the letter which Bowes addressed to the Editor of the Morning print, and after having pointed out to the observation of the reader, that, as he has seen in a former letter, that Bowes had, as I said, retained Eliza in his service, so he has in this letter applied, as his tool, one of the Countess's male literati, Mr. MATRA, for his service also, and that in a situation which is judged to be of a serious and confidential nature.

LETTER FROM A. R. S. TO THE REV. MR. B.

St. James's Street, 12*th Jan.* 1777.

As you seem determined, from what motives is best known to yourself, not to allow my FRIEND, MR. MATRA, to settle the disagreeable transaction that now subsists between us, I desire to know where you are to be found this evening at eight o'clock, as I intend to give you every kind of provocation till I can bring you to a proper sense of your conduct.

I am, Sir,

Your humble servant,

A. ROBINSON S.

P. S. As you appear to be timorously inclined, I give you my honor I shall go alone, and shall not bring any implements of war with me. I am engaged to dine with a gentleman at the Cocoa Tree, but shall not have it in my power to get away before the hour I have fixed

The above letter was sent on the Sunday, and on the subsequent day the RENCONTRE took place, of which I am now about to give a statement.

A NARRATIVE OF THE RENCONTRE.

It was on Monday evening, on the 13th of January, 1777, that I was called upon by a gentleman whom I personally knew, in great haste, to come to the Adelphi Tavern. The reason, I suppose, why I was pitched upon, was my vicinity to the spot, as my residence then was in Salisbury Street, which is the nearest street to the Adelphi. I was brought into a room, where I saw·the Editor, Mr. B----- whom I only knew personally, Mr. Bowes, whom I had never seen before, another stranger, and Doctor Scott, who resided in John Street, Adelphi; besides a servant, I think these were all the persons I first saw there. Bowes was sitting on a chair with his collar unbuttoned, throwing himself back, and was assisted by smelling bottles, and wine and water, He looked very pale, and I thought ready to faint. He attracted my attention most; and after speaking to his opponent, and enquiring from himself, the nature of

his wound, he recommended me to look to Bowes,
as his own was not of this serious importance.
This gallant conduct sent me to Bowes; and upon
examination I saw the wound on his right breast,
from whence the blood was then trickling: upon a
closer inspection, I saw two wounds on the substance of the right breast, about four inches dis-
tance from each other, in an oblique line with each
other. As I was given to understand that swords
had been used as well as pistols, and as I saw the
swords, one of which had been bent, I never have
had any other opinion, but that these two wounds
on the breast were made by the point of the sword
passing in at the one and coming out at the other.
There was another wound, but not so important.
His opponent was also wounded; and by the
wound being externally on the right thigh, it excited considerable pain, from the anatomical nature
of the part; and though not dangerous, required
rest and care to prevent inflammation.

After having temporarily applied something to
the wounds of both, I went away with Bowes in
his vis-avis, and called on Sir Cæsar Hawkins, in
Pall Mall, in our way to the St. James's Coffee
House, who promised to be there by the time I
could prepare the necessary articles for more effec-
tually dressing the wounds. Sir Cæsar came to
his time; and after examining the wounds with his
probe, they were dressed. Sir Cæsar saw Bowes
again the next day, and attended him on with me
till the wounds were healed. Sir Cæsar also saw
Mr. B----- the next day, with me, and I remember

particularly seeing Mr. Garrick there, as Mr. B--'s
residence then was also in the Adelphi. I did not
forget to say, that the looking-glass in the room
was broken all to pieces, which I understood was
done by the ball of a pistol.

This is what I have to say about this rencontre,
and the wounds that were received by both the
duellists. But the friends of the late Lord S----,
and those of Mr. Gray, would not permit the report of the rencontre, as it was given in one of the
papers, to pass without a criticism upon it in another paper, in which too much was attempted to
be done away, or, perhaps, their criticism might
have been at the time more successful. They not
only denied there having been a real duel, but also
denied the wounds. And I have heard a discarded
servant of Bowes's SWEAR TWICE, in the Court of
Common Pleas, once before Lord Loughborough
twenty-three years ago, and since, in 1807, before
Sir James Mansfield, that there were no wounds;
that the shirt Bowes had on, and his clothes, had
neither holes or blood. I have heard this repeated
at both these trials; and when the evidence of this
servant was given to this very purpose in the year
1807, the Editor, Mr. B----, was there, and feeling, as he did, the insult that was offered, called
upon the Court to examine him, and confront him
with this protected witness. But he did not obtain
a hearing, nor was I examined. I think this a
curious anecdote of the law; but I am happy that it
raises in me no other emotion, but contemplating it
as a curious anecdote of the law.

Had those who doubted the fact of there having been a serious 'rencontre, detached the doubt of a serious rencontre from the actual wounds, as the one could not be proved, but the other could, they would have acted more politic; whereas, by denying both, they could be contradicted by proof; for if one was false and the other was true, they having confounded them together made them more readily credited to be both true. All that I know of the matter is, that the wounds, as I have stated them, were described from ocular demonstration.'

I will now copy what appeared in the paper called the GAZETTEER, in consequence of the report of its not having been a serious rencontre, and of 'there having been no wounds. As it will be seen by the date, this came out after Bowes was married.

GAZETTEER, Friday, January 24, 1777.

' A Morning Paper having misrepresented the circumstances of a late duel which happened at the Adelphi Tavern, from the mischievous intention of an anonymous correspondent, has this day, in justice to the gentlemen concerned, ingenuously confessed the error into which it was led, and published the following

ATTESTATION.

We whose names are subscribed, were called within a few minutes after the rencontre that happened at the Adelphi Tavern, on Monday the 13th instant, and found A. Robinson S-----, Esq. and the Rev. Mr. B-----,* both wounded, the former in his right breast, through which the sword of his antagonist had obliquely passed, which bled very considerably, besides another small wound directly above; there was also a slight wound in the right arm.

The latter was wounded on the external part of the right thigh, which, on account of its situation, was soon much inflamed. He had also a slight wound on the abdomen; and we have every reason to believe that the rencontre must have determined fatally, had not the interposition of the gentleman who broke into the room put an end to it.

JOHN SCOTT, M. D.
JESSE FOOT.

January 22, 1777.

To the above account, as signed by Dr. Scott and Mr. Foot, Sir Cæsar Hawkins, who saw Mr. S----- in consultation with Mr. Foot about two hours after the rencontre, and likewise visited Mr. B-----, with Mr. Foot, the morning following subscribes his attestation.

C. HAWKINS.

Pall Mall, January 22, 1777,

COPY.

The following is what I know of the late affair of honour between Mr. B---- and Capt. S---. Being in a room above stairs, at the Adelphi Tavern, on Monday evening, the *13th* instant, about six o'clock, as I was reading the newspaper, I heard a noise like the report of a pistol, and presently after another; I did not at that instant apprehend it was the discharge of a pistol, but the violent shutting too of a door, till some minutes after, when I heard a noise as of two persons fencing; this being so very violent, alarmed me, as I thought it impossible to be play, therefore immediately ran down stairs, when I found my fears were well founded; for after some time, with the assistance of the waiters, the door was burst open, when, upon rushing in, I seized upon Capt. S----'s sword arm, and immediately threw myself before him, for fear he should receive any further hurt from his antagonist, whom I presently saw was Mr. B-----, whose behaviour at that instant convinced me, that no further danger was to be apprehended from him. Soon afterwards, therefore, (though with no small difficulty) I prevailed upon Capt. S----- to yield me up his sword: and as he at that time seemed to be very weak, I apprehended he was hurt, and upon my examining him I found he was much wounded; I think there were three wounds in his right breast, and one upon his sword arm. Mr. Foot, the surgeon, seemed to think one of the former may be dangerous.

It was matter of great surprize to me, that one or other of the combatants were not absolutely killed on the spot, as I found them, on my entering, in the dark, the candles having been knocked down,

as I suppose, in the engagement. Capt. S——
fainted twice, but whether, it was from loss ·of
blood, (which was considerable,) or from the violent agitation of his spirits, I am not able to judge.
I cannot but observe that Capt. S?----- was very·par-
ticular in acquitting Mr. B----- of any ungentleman-
like behaviour during the whole affair, and repeatedly advised him to make his escape in his carriage,
for fear of any fatal consequence attending him.

(Signed)   J. HULL.

Salt Office, Wednesday, 3 *o'clock.*

The only remark I shall make as to the fact of
the wounds is, that here are four witnesses, Dr.
Scott, Sir Cæsar Hawkins, Mr. Hull, and myself.
Four such witnesses would serve to attest the con-
veyance of the largest property that ever was
sold; would bring condemnation on a criminal,
or acquit an innocent; would be equal to the intention of ratifying the most solemn acts of property, of life, and of death.

The purpose of the trial, when the witness I
allude to was called to prove that Bowes was not
wounded, was to recover estates made over to
Bowes by the Countess in May, 1777, a few months
after their marriage, in order that he might raise
money upon them; and when the Countess escaped
from Bowes in the year 1785, and swore the peace
against him, these estates were claimed from Bowes,
founded upon the proof, that they were obtained
from her not with her fair consent, but by ill usage
and compulsion.

- In trying this question, the lawyers began with the duel; and though there were evidences enough to establish Bowes's tortures and cruelties towards the Countess, yet they were not content with these, but opened their cause with this duel, which was a circumstance before the marriage. As this witness could have been contradicted, and the cases of tortures and cruelties could not, perhaps could not for want of proof, it was the more necessary that this witness should have been contradicted, as it would have tended to invalidate, or at least to weaken the force of the rest of the witnesses; for all the witnesses were much of the same class with this one. I am apt to think also, that up to the month of May, of the same year they were married, Bowes HAD NOT TREATED HER WITH SO MUCH BRUTALITY as he did afterwards. Bowes then had two pressing concerns upon him, to conceal the state of the Countess's health, and to satisfy Mr. Gray by giving him hush money.

For the purpose of stopping Mr. Gray's action, which he had given notice of, and to pay debts contracted before marriage, he wanted to raise a sum of money upon annuities. The Countess was at the Royal Exchange UPON VIEW for many days, and, IN MY OPINION, consented without restraint in this transaction, if she ever did in any one, after her fatal marriage. Bowes saw the necessity of getting over this business as early as he could, on account of her HEALTH. There was some grace in this; Bowes was not now entirely lost to all sense of honour. When he married the Countess, he took her as she was, and nothing then stood in his way, but after marriage, he wished to keep her secrets, not for her's, but his own sake, and for his own reputation. What Bowes wanted was, that every thing should pass for his own, and that is the reason why he made the Countess say worse things in the CONFESSIONS, and which did not trench upon his interest. The money was raised, and Mr. Gray received £12,000 of it.

Having said as much as I think necessary about the DUEL, and having followed the consequences of it beyond the time that the marriage took place, on purpose to give a more full explanation, I shall now return to Bowes and the Countess, and state what they were doing about the time of the duel.

The Countess having been worked upon by the continued attacks in the Morning Paper upon her, was heard to declare to Miss P-------, that the man who would call upon the Editor of that Paper, and revenge her cause upon him, should have both her hand and her heart. The object was found to be from this expression fast approaching to a successful conclusion; and Bowes had triumphed over his rival.

Mr. Gray called on Bowes the morning after the duel, shook him heartily by the hand, thanked him, and expressed himself full of gratitude to him; it is plain from this, that he was not in the smallest degree aware that Bowes would be ever married to the Countess.

Here then let us pause to contemplate the life of the Countess within these last NINE MONTHS, and let us reflect upon the state in which she was, and is now to be seen. She whose wealth and education and connections commanded all the attention, and all the abilities which instruction can obtain through money; let us reflect that she is a mother, and that she brought forth five children by her late Lord, and to what an end her state is come at last. Then let us turn our attention to an opposite picture, to one the reverse, and of the same sex, to one who possesses native sweetness, innocence, modesty, mildness and affection, to one whose mind has not been vitiated, and who adorns and maintains her rank in nature as the highest for admiration of any thing created. The Italian Marquis who was the Countess's CHAPERON for twelve months, the Governesses from the Museum, the social friends Mr. Matra, and Mr. Magra introduced by Doctor Solander, the Domestic Chaplain, the vast income, the castles and houses, have all but served to disfigure the native perfection of a woman, and to give her the appearance of a fallen angel.

The Countess's possessions then were, her house and garden at Chelsea, with conservatories and hothouses, upon the largest scale, her house in Grosvenor Square, her seats at Paul's Walden, Gibside, Streatham Castle, and Barnard Castle, besides lands in Middlesex

On the morning after the duel, Bowes's apartments were filled with visitors; and the expectation

he had promised as the result of the duel, kept him
in a constant state of agitation until the day of the
marriage. He knew the fickleness, of her nature,
and hurried on the day as fast as possible, that day
which gave her no other choice in life but repentance, a privilege which she was certain to stand in
need of.

On the 17th of January, four days after the duel,
Bowes and the Countess were married at St.
James's Church, by the Rev. Mr. Gardiner, to
whom he gave £50, and in a few days afterwards
he took possession of the house and all the MOVE-
ABLES in Grosvenor Square.

Here, then, are joined in holy wedlock, two such
as for the honour of human nature are seldom to be
found. The one had broken the heart of a former
wife, the other had not lengthened the days of a
former husband; in a battle-royal of a main of
cocks, the two surviving ones contend for existence,
and thus are these two pitted as by positive destina-
tion.

Soon after the marriage, Bowes addressed a
GOOD letter to his mother-in-law, Mrs. Bowes, then
residing at Paul's Walden, of which the following
are the contents :---

MADAM,

It is not more my duty, than it is my inclination
to remove as far as it comes within my power, the

uneasiness which the unexpected intelligence to
you of my marriage with Lady Strathmore must
have occasioned. Had it been possible for me to
have flattered myself with your approbation, my
happiness upon the occasion would have been complete; but as I could not convey to you the state
of mind and honour and integrity of my intention,
which were my chief advocates with Lady Strathmore, I was under the necessity of violating a ceremony, which my inclinations strongly dictated to
me to comply with, and celebrated a marriage without your concurrence. Deeply impressed with the
sense of the impropriety that may appear to you for
my conduct, I wish to atone for that breach of duty,
and to ask your pardon under the promise of dedi-
cating the remainder of my life to the honour and
interest of your daughter and her family. My
grateful heart will make me her faithful companion,
and with unremitting attention I will consult her
peace of mind, and the advantage of the children.

My situation and family connections give me the
pleasing prospect of domestic happiness, and I hope
the introduction of my friend to the honour of an
intimacy in your family will be approved and attended with those advantages which are found from
receiving good company.

I shall study to deserve the honour and unlimited
confidence which has been placed in me, and by an
exact obedience to your inclinations, I shall be
happy to regulate my conduct, so as to merit your

approbation; and under the idea that I may hereafter be admitted to your friendship, I beg permission with respect to subscribe,

Your affectionate humble Servant,
ANDREW ROBINSON BOWES.

MRS. BOWES did not long survive the shock of
this marriage and her daughter's conduct. She was
a truly good and charitable woman; indeed her
charity was indiscreet, as Paul's Walden lies out
of the common road, the beggars which flocked
there infested the parish; she gave food, clothing,
and lodging to all who came.

The morning after Bowes's marriage, he had
quite a levee; not being well enough to be moved,
or not now caring much about it, he was seen
dressed in a new suit of regimentals; his vanity re-
minding him, that fourteen years ago, he was the
youngest Lieutenant upon half pay of a disbanded
regiment. Two General Officers in their full regimental dresses paid him and the Countess the nup-
tial visit; these were his near relations; General
Robinson of Marlborough street, and General Armstrong of Berners street. General Lambton called
in his regimental dress also; he was the relation
of the Countess. In point of family and origin,
the couple were much upon a par, I never could see
much difference between them.

The cards were in heaps that were left by visitors
in coaches, on horseback, and on foot; all was bus-

tle; and there would have been something light and airy, something of felicity in this knight-errand frolick of Fortune, something which on a superficial mind would strike the attention, as a prosperous and dexterous piece of romance; but the foundation was not sound; the cause was not good; the prospect was not bright; the back ground was sombrous; the light had no warmth, it was like the luminous appearance emitted from rotten wood in a dark night; the perfume was not sweet-scented; no bride-maids graced the nuptials; Hymen's torch burnt not clear, and the Countess from henceforth may truly be pronounced to be DEAD ALIVE.

NON REDOLET SED OLET, QUÆ REDOLERE SOLET.

After the married couple removed to Grosvenor Square, Bowes opened the scene, and gave a few grand dinners to those who would attend them; and after the house had undergone the change naturally to be expected from folly to tyranny, the females which had been first dishonoured, were next discarded, and all his other instruments the male literati having served his turn, and done his business completely, were sent adrift also. He invited the faculty to a dinner, amongst whom was the Countess's Surgeon, Mr. John Hunter, he had seen the wounds on their second dressing.

Here, then, every thing relative to the marriage was about to close, and when he had presented the Countess to the underwriters, and raised the money, Grosvenor Square soon became deserted.

Within a month of his marriage, Sir Walter
Blacket, a Member for Newcastle, died; Bowes
offered himself as a candidate, assigning ill health
for not personally canvassing the voters.   He stood
the contest against Sir John Trevelyan, and he pe-
titioned the House of Commons, but finally lost his
election.

Doctor Scott, who was present just after the
duel, resided in the Adelphi, where he had a sort
of Dispensary; and his wife was a very nice and
well-disposed woman.   The Doctor (Scott) promised from a certain smartness and plausibility, to
become a useful new instrument to Bowes; the
Doctor had the honour of being appointed his Physician; he obtained all his confidence; and he was
well informed of the Countess's state of health.

Bowes took a house at Hammersmith, to which
she retired; It was a house the Margravine of An-
spach had left, quite secluded from the busy pry-
ing eye of curiosity, and where Bowes might hear
the cuckoo in the merry month of May, the time
they went there, without its being unwelcome to the
married ear.

By his taking this house, it was very clear that
the house in the Square, or that at Chelsea, or that at
Paul's Walden, would not suit their purpose so
well; and here they remained some considerable
time, and his Physician also.

At the expiration of three months, they quitted

this snug retreat at Hammersmith, and made a journey to their possessions in the North. Bowes not forgetting even there, to take also HIS Physician.

On the Countess's arrival at GIBSIDE, her ancient domain, an accoucheur was sent for, and directed to be in waiting, as the Countess expected every hour to call out for his assistance; but whether he was pleased to be too slow, or the Countess was pleased to be too much in haste, or whether Bowes was pleased to govern the will of both, the child was born alive and well before the arrival of the accoucheur, and the Countess was in a very fine sleep. The tardy accoucheur took his fee and his departure.

The twelve thousand pounds paid to Mr. Gray, was raised in May, when the Countess possessed Bowes of the property which was said to be obtained by compulsion. The deed was witnessed by Doctor Scott, not the Doctor Scott lately spoken of, but by the Rev. Doctor Scott, the writer of the letters signed ANTE SEJANUS, during the time of the Earl of Sandwich being at the head of the Admiralty.

If any part of this extraordinary character excited more than common curiosity, it would be, I imagine, by speculating how Bowes would conduct himself after coming into so vast a fortune. In the intrigue he carried on to obtain the Countess, by ousting Mr. Gray, he evidently evinced 'a superio-

rity over him, and at a time when any other man
would have given up all prospect of hope of success from the priority of advantage in the possession of Mr. Gray. Both of them tried to obtain
the Countess by guilty means; and one may be
punished by another, who is as guilty as himself,
and who has also combined in the profanation of all
sacred duties.

And though the mode Bowes took to obtain the
Countess was that of an impostor, yet if he had
conducted himself like a man, and treated her well
afterwards, he might have been pardoned and acquitted; if he had acted like LEON in the comedy
of RULE A WIFE AND HAVE A WIFE, after his marriage, like LEON, he might have been applauded.

Before I see what Bowes is about in the North,
I will first of all settle his account of his conduct
during the summer in town, independent of his
election concern, and of his Hammersmith MYS-
TERY.

Bowes and the Editor of the Morning Print, had
a revived quarrel of a very serious nature, and
which threatened extreme consequences, the account of which I shall here give with as much accu-
racy and impartiality as I possibly can.

Bowes having publicly read the following
letter (subscribed with the initials of his name) to
the members of the Cocoa Tree; the gentleman to
whom it was addressed, not having the honour of

being a member of that Society, found it impossible
to do himself justice, but by the publication of his
answer to it, which Bowes, it seems, did not read,
and stating at the same time the grounds of this
new correspondence.

About six weeks ago, Mr. B----- was informed
that Bowes had publicly declared at one of the
clubs, " that he (Mr. B-----) was very short-sighted
in their late affair, or he might have perceived the
views he had in calling him to an account." Naturally hurt at the bare idea of such a reflection coming from Mr. Bowes, Mr. B----- wrote a very civil
note to him, only requesting to know whether the
information he had received, was true? but to which
he received no answer. A few days afterwards, a
second note of a similar nature was sent; but no
answer: a third succeeded it of a more spirited nature, in which an explanation was insisted upon, or
his silence would be deemed a confession of his
guilt. To this he thought proper to deliver the following laconic answer to the chairman who carried
it---" Tell the gentleman I wear a sword!" Mortified not a little on the receipt of this message, Mr.
B----- waited upon him in Grosvenor Square the
next morning, attended by a gentleman, but was
told he was not at home: the porter was asked
what was the most probable time to meet with his
master? He replied about twelve. Mr. B----- then
gave him a card, and said, " Tell your master the
gentleman whose name is on the card, will call
upon him to-morrow precisely at twelve." Mr.
B----- was in Grosvenor Square the next day at the

hour appointed. but was informed that Mr. Bowes was neither at home, nor had he left any message. Mr. B----- irritated at this treatment, desired him to tell his master, " that though he had so studiously avoided him, he was determined to see him at all events." He therefore repeated his visits the next day, but with no more success than before. It happened immediately upon this, that the fracas behind the scenes at the Haymarket broke out. Mr. B----- thinking this might afford him an opportunity to bring Bowes to a proper explanation, made himself master of the facts, and sent them to a newspaper, with a determination of avowing himself the author of the article, whenever called upon. This produced the following letter :---

COPY.

Monday Morning.

SIR,

I have known bad men, I have heard of many, and have been a dissipated man myself, but of all the diabolical wretches that since the beginning of the world, God thought expedient to introduce upon earth, as a detested example of vile prodigality, you are the first. A man who exists without a possibility of having one flattering thought, even to be extracted from the pinnacle of ideal fiction, except that of being conscious of never nearly having an equal, not so much as excluding those who have suffered from the just laws of their country.

Providence, when we last met, thought you too proper a subject for public justice, to allow you to fall for the satisfaction of an individual, has therefore, I presume, detained you as an example and partner in clerical reprobation; ·else what devil could have instructed you to have made a second attack upon me, when you know I wish to relinquish every part of the world that can produce so infernal and black a book, AS YOUR COUNTENANCE.

I am, &c.

R. B.

P S.   I have advised you before to let me alone, I give you the same now.   I did not think proper to answer your letter, nor to be at home when you called, because I did not wish to get into a second quarrel with you ; however, lest you should think me afraid of you, which is a character I dislike as much as that of being too forward, I shall be at home till six o'clock this evening, and·after that period shall be at the theatre.   The account you have given about my being drunk the other night at the theatre is in part true, though most of it is false, and therefore calls my resentment : the other paragraph is totally so, but of no consequence.   Take care you don't extend matters too far ; your prerogative is now upon the stretch, shamefully so indeed.

Since I wrote the above, I have determined to be at home till seven o'clock.

To the Rev. Mr. B-----, Adelphi.

To which was immediately sent back the underwritten answer :---

COPY.

Monday noon.

SIR,

I HAVE just received a letter signed R. B. which, from its bedlamite strains, I conceive to be the genuine effusions of your extraordinary head and heart. The man, however, who dares to hold the language to me, which I have been able to collect from the only intelligible part of it, is a liar and a scoundrel. What you mean by expecting me at your house this evening, after the very singular line of conduct you have lately pursued, I neither know nor care; but I am now advised not to be imprudent enough to enter under the roof of an assassin. I shall therefore take the opportunity of expressing my sentiments of you in the face of the world.

Why do you upbraid me for those disagreeable reflections, which your conscience has called up upon the perusal of the papers of this day? You had better, Mr. S-----, endeavour, by honest and honourable means, to stifle those self-reproaches, than calumniate the man with so much virulence to whom, through accident, in all probability, you owe every thing you now possess.

If the Morning Post has published any thing against you that is untrue, I will call the printer to an account for it, and make him do you ample justice; further than this your late behaviour con-vinces me you have no right to expect at my hands. Your going to the theatre this evening may possibly be in order to raise a fresh disturbance at that house. I shall be there likewise, though with no such intention.

Yours, &c.

H. B.

To R. Bowes, Grosvenor Square.

Some days elapsed before any further notice was taken of this matter by Bowes, till some other ar-ticles were announced in the papers for publication, when Bowes deputed the Rev. Mr. Maxwell, of the kingdom of Ireland, to wait upon his antago-nist, to endeavour to smother, or rather fence with him, in which, however, he did not succeed. He was told, it was expected that BOWES would give him an assurance that he did not cast any reflec-tion upon him, and that he would make him a pro-per apology. Through the subsequent mediation of MR. WILKINSON, then Bowes's solicitor, an ac-commodation was at length effected, under the arbitrament of two gentlemen on each side, who decided, THAT BOWES SHOULD MAKE A PROPER APOLOGY FOR HIS EXTRAORDINARY CONDUCT.

Bowes looked out for a CHAPLAIN to his family, and appears to have been nicely scrupulous in the selection. Many candidates offered. He has told us from his extreme critical situation in point of public approbation, that he could not be too minute in his enquiries about those who are to be admitted to his house and confidence.

On his going to the north, in the autumn, when the Countess accompanied him to lie in there; then it was that he began to shew himself, as to the application of the immense property which had, by his marriage, fallen to him. GIBSIDE is remarkable for rich and extensive plantations of valuable woods; and whether Bowes had the power, by law of cutting down timber or not, here, within ten months of his marriage, is a letter from this plundering adventurer, which, besides the timber, includes the subject of more annuities.

LETTER I.

From Andrew Robinson Bowes, Esq. to ------ ----- -----, Esq.

GIBSIDE, *November* 7, 1778.

Yesterday I received your letter, and am extremely sorry to hear of your indisposition. I shall be very glad to see the TIMBER MERCHANT, and shall have no difference with him about the time of payment, nor I dare say about the prices; but as for paying him the expence of his journey, it is such a proposal never was heard in this country, or, I believe, any other. It is just as much as to say, I will run the chance of making a great bargain, without suffering the least risk. If you will be so obliging as to have my wood put into any of the papers, I am sure of fifty bidders, without any expence. It has never been offered to sale; and I will venture to say, SUCH WOOD IS NOT IN ENG-LAND, at least in any one place, his Majesty's Docks excepted. The Dock Company in this country has made me a great offer, in order TO SELL AGAIN; but I have been told the people in London can afford to give more, how true remains to be proved.

I am obliged to you for the trouble you have had about the insurance, and beg you will send me a list of a few of the best brokers in London. I will see myself and them damned before I agree to the price you mention. D----, when I was last in town, got me £3000. much under that charge.

I am ever yours,

A. R. BOWES.

> P. S. If you see the wood matter in a diffe-rent light, I leave it to you.

In four days after Bowes had signed the con-demnation of the fine woods at GIBSIDE, he opened another vein of peculation, or rather enlarged upon what he had first began. This letter is dated from COAL PIG HILL, the ancient property of the NEWTONS, his first wife.

The ebullitions of his vanity are here to be seen rising very fast.

LETTER II.

From the same to the same.

CoAL PIG HILL, *November* 11, 1778.

Though I am this moment going out a hunting, I must write one line to answer your obliging letter of the 4th instant. I am much obliged by the information you give me relative to the new CREATION *. I was before too apprehensive the power was in the option of the ministers, and that the difficulty therefore would be great in my PRESENT situation. However, my dear friend, time should be always taken by the forelock, and hope, on that account, a trifle (of five hundred pounds for instance) will not allow you to stop your proceedings. I came here last Sunday, with my wife and sister, and General B-----, upon a hunting party; the W------ns are to be here to-day. My real reason was to avoid the sore throat, which was very troublesome at GIBSIDE, though, thank God, not mortal. Markam, (my chaplain,) his wife, and Major P----, KEEPS house. We RETURN on Sunday. The last policies that were done for me, WAS by D-----, at six per cent. for two years, the hand of justice and suicide excepted. I will send to you when I return, in order to have the names examined. The other policies you mention in your last letter ONLY shall be sent to you the moment I return to GIBSIDE, with your promise, that they

---

* By creation, he means a title.

shall be returned immediately, as I believe you
will find names on them that ought not to be there.
The hint you gave me about Mr. W----- would be
very pleasing to me, you may be assured, but I
must know nothing yet.

   I am,

     Dear Sir,

       In much hurry, yours, &c.

         A. R. Bowes.

  P S. If ten thousand can be accomplished
  upon the above terms, I will give my note
  payable in two months when finished.

  If I should ever get into parliament, I shall
  have plenty of things to ask, without waiting for the matter in question.

 Such are the after-thoughts of a man who con-
cludes his letter in a HURRY. The venerable steward
of the family, who I remember to have once seen
in his scarlet and gold waistcoat, was made, by
Bowes, to remit to this same correspondent all the
money he could muster, to the amount of some
thousands, as his banker in town did not choose to
contribute, at his own risk, to Bowes's vanity.
This banker will be abused by him.

LETTER III.

From the same to the same.

GIBSIDE, *December* 15th, 1778.

I was last night favoured with yours of the 9th instant, and this morning wrote to Mr. Gibson, to answer that part of it relative to Mr. G-----.   I am sorry you have had so much trouble about the insurance; I will not give sixpence more than six guineas, and think even that shamefully exorbitant, as for one year the price I paid before was only three pounds ten.   Pray is -----'s BANK still existing?   I cannot get a letter from them; though between the 4th of September and 27th of November, Gibson has remitted them £3950. and they may expect to receive £1000. more in the course of this month.

I am yours sincerely,

A. R. BOWES.

P. S. I have given up all idea of going this winter to London, as I can live here for half the expence; besides, I never can be happy TILL I GET OUT OF DEBT, and have money, if possible, to the good.

The purpose of this last paragraph was to get the confidence and the credit of this correspondent more readily at his command, as will be seen in his two next letters after his return to London, in

the month of May, 1789, when THE HOUSE, THE HOT
HOUSE, AND CONSERVATORIES AT CHELSEA, WILL ALL
GO.

LETTER IV.

From the same to the same.

NEWMARKET, *April* 29, 1779.

I beg you will assist Mr. G----- in preventing the
annuitants from taking any disagreeable step till
my arrival in town, on Monday; and you may
add, that they shall call to be paid the ensuing
week, and never have occasion to complain in
future.

I am yours sincerely,

A. R. BOWES.

WALKER is out of danger from his fall yesterday, which was at first thought mortal.

LETTER V.

From the same to the same.

GROSVENOR SQUARE, *May* 10, 1779.

I called on you this morning, according to my
general mode, to ask a favour. In short, my
banker has been so uncommonly pressing, that it
is impossible for me ever to ask him another favour,
or to lose more time than I can help in liquidating

every account between us, which I shall do very
expeditiously after my arrival in the north. I have
lately paid into his bank upwards of £2000. and
shall soon totally get free of him, for reasons I shall
mention more freely to you when we meet.

All the favour I have to ask of you is, that you
will procure me time, for a few weeks more, for
the payment of my note, in your favour; and if I
was obliged (which will not be the case) to sell
the chair I sit on, by God, it should be done. I
HAVE SOLD CHELSEA HOUSE, but have not got the
money; which, however, when I do, must go to
-----, the banker.

I am sincerely yours,
A. R. BOWES

In the month of June, with all his shiftings for
money, he purchased a race horse, and went upon
the turf: the name of the horse was ICELANDER,
which he pretended to his friend only to buy to
sell again.

LETTER VI.

From the same to the same.

GIBSIDE, June 28, 1779.

Nothing but absolute necessity could have induced me to be again troublesome, when I am
already so much indebted to you for your assistance and kind readiness to oblige me in all money

transactions. Nothing could give me greater pleasure than to have an opportunity of shewing my
just sense of the obligation I am under. The
favour I have to request is, that as both my bills
will be soon due, you will keep one of them in
your hands a short time longer, and contrive to
pay the other by the enclosed bill, which is accepted by the Duke of A-----. Till I receive my
rents, I find it will be impossible for me to be
easier in my pecuniary transactions. In performing this you will do me a singular service, and
give me a most acceptable proof of your friendship.

I am sincerely yours,
A. R. Bowes.

P. S. My mare walked over, consequently
you win your bet from the General. Or-
pheus was backed to him ten to one against
the field; but Icelander run him, the last
heat, within half a neck; the finest race I
ever saw.

In the following month he wrote to this old
friend the following letter:---

LETTER VII.

From the same to the same.

GROSVENOR SQUARE, *July* 6, 1779.

As I well know by my own experience, (a fact which few would credit,) that it is impossible to pronounce who is at present in a state of affluence, I shall not acknowledge that I think you have acted in an unfriendly manner; but I cannot avoid observing, that I did not expect a refusal of my request, even though from any body else I had no right to expect it would be granted. There is not the most distant prospect of your suffering finally from me; a period not very remote must finally reimburse you. At this moment, I declare, I am worth, were all effects sold, above £50,000, which no casualties can influence. I confess I have often promised, and intended, to discharge your demands, but have been obliged to disappoint you, from unexpected events; for instance, not being able to sell my wood, receive my rent, &c. &c. My banker can but too fully tell you of my uncomfortable situation. It is impossible, were my life at stake, to raise the sum as soon as it will be due, and that I would compound with resigning to the old gentleman in the Red Sea, you and all, and

Your sincere friend,

A. R. BOWES.

LETTER VIII.

From the same to the same.

GIBSIDE, *February* 11, 1780.

I received your letter in due time, and determined to answer it every day, but my time has
been lately so fully engrossed by our patriotic
meetings, and their APPENDAGES, that it had deprived me of the pleasure of writing to you sooner;
besides, to confess the truth, your silence rather
created some jealousies in my mind; this circumstance, however, I now doubt not, was solely occasioned by a point of delicacy.

I am now, thank God, so far advanced in my
affairs, as to have quite discharged my debt to my
bankers, whose behaviour HAVE been so very un-
gentlemanlike and displeasing to me, that I mean
to break off all connection with them the moment
I can bite, which I expect will be very soon; and
till then it would be folly to shew my teeth.

The people who have mortgages upon my estates
continue harassing me incessantly; but even these
great difficulties I have nearly got over, by mere
frugality. To convince you how sincere I am in
my desire to acquit myself of some part of my
obligations to you, I shall make an offer, which I
take it may not prove inconvenient to you to accept.

There is an estate of about £400 per annum, near BARNARD CASTLE, entirely in my own disposal, and has no incumbrance upon it, excepting £2000 I owe to Mr. Peel, of Symond's Inn, the interest of which has been duly paid. If this purchase suits you, I shall be glad, as it is the only method I can think of at PRESENT to accommodate you; and I dare say we shall not differ about the price.

> I am,
>> Your sincere and obliged friend,
>> A. R. BOWES.

P. S. Between ourselves, I assure you, that you may bet any sum you please that I am MEMBER for NEWCASTLE, without the least opposition; this, well managed, something may be done. You may back ICELANDER at the next meeting, provided you make it play or pay.

LETTER IX.

From the same to the same,

GIBSIDE, *February* 29, 1780.

An affidavit of the value of the estate, I find upon enquiry, was made the other day, in order to procure more time for the payment of the £2000 upon it. Chancery has allowed me six months longer. It only amounts, at present, to £330 per annum; but am told it may be let for near one hundred more. It is a freehold estate, and was bought after the death of the late Mr. B-----, at thirty-five years purchase, but then let at only £300; so that I should take considerable less. I own it is a great hardship upon you to insure Lady S-----'s life, particularly as you are not paid regularly; but, considering all things, I think you should not throw away your money in that way: a better life cannot be; and, at any rate, you can be nothing out of pocket. I am glad to find the opinions of people in London against my election; it will give you an opportunity of making some good bets; and so positive am I, that I have no objection to your standing a third part to nothing, and you may make me liable to pay the whole in case I should not succeed. But you must bet upon a proviso, that L---- S----- lives.

F-----, of Benwell, and a set of foxhunters, are now here with their hounds, so that I must defer several particulars that I had to mention to you till another opportunity, as I have not one moment to myself. F----- desires his compliments, as I am writing to you on the dinner table.

I am yours sincerely,

A. R. BOWES.

LETTER X.

From the same to the same.

GIBSIDE, *August,* 1780.

You may be assured that the purchase you have made will, in every essential, turn out cheap. The canvass is begun at Newcastle---three candidates, all upon different interests: for God's sake use your influence with as many people of the WHOLE in the Wall as you possibly can find out, and pray use ANY MEANS to procure them for me. Excuse the hurry of a canvass.

Yours sincerely,

A. R. BOWES.

Five o'clock, Wednesday Morning.

LETTER XI.

From the same to the same.

GIBSIDE, *August* 11, 1781.

I am very uneasy at not having heard from you since your last obliging letter, wherein you say that you have engaged a new person to insure Lady S-----'s life, at three guineas, and wherein you mention that a Mr. W--- has already done Lady S-----'s life to a great amount. As to Mr. W-----, he never had any orders from me to that effect, for those last two years, consequently, I presume, it must have been for some of the annuitants. I shall take it as a favour if you will direct the persons you employ in this business to write to me occasionally, to mention what progress they make, as well as to send me a list of the names they may have procured; for though Lady Strathmore is in PERFECT HEALTH, yet as she is with child, I am determined to insure her life deeply, if I can do it for three guineas; and I trust that you will use your utmost to have this matter properly accomplished for me with all possible expedition. We are all well, and set off for the Moors the 15th instant, therefore direct your letters in future to me at STREATLAM CASTLE, near BARNARD CASTLE. I apprehend you will not keep your word relative to visiting me this summer; Mrs. -----, I presume, will not allow it.

I am, in a hurry, sincerely yours,

A. R. BOWES.

P. S. Pray find out the particulars relative to Mr. W-----'s insuring.

LETTER XII.

From the same to the same.

STREATLAM CASTLE, *August* 30, 1781.

I am very uneasy that you have not written to me lately about the insurances upon Lady Strathmore's life. Pray do not now neglect me, or you will oblige me to take a London journey, which at this time would be very troublesome to me. Lady

S----- is in PERFECT HEALTH; but I have many reasons for desiring you to lose no time.

I am yours sincerely,

A. R. BOWES.

LETTER XIII.

From the same to the same.

STREATLAM CASTLE, *September* 2, 1781.

I am thankful for your last letter, but am much disappointed that you have not been able to get the business accomplished. I have received a letter from Messrs. R----- and K-----; they have only done six hundred pounds, and seem anxious for the old policies, which I cannot send them, as I have left them either at GIBSIDE or in town; but I think you may easily get a copy of the names that were upon them from Mr. G-----. The suc cess of policies of this kind chiefly depends upon the interest the broker has with underwriters.

Lady Strathmore is in perfect health; but as I have reason to think she is with child, nay, I am certain of it, I wish to insure her life, for you remember HOW ALARMED I WAS UPON A FORMER OCCASION *; though, indeed, I ought not to have much reason for it, as she always recovered vastly

---

* If this gentleman is to remember that Bowes was alarmed upon a former occasion, that occasion must have been in the vicinity of London then, as I am confident the gentleman did not accompany, precede, or follow, the family to GIBSIDE. I. F.

well. However, I request you will immediately exert yourself for me, and get the £18,000 filled with good names. I presume there is no occasion to say any thing about her being with child. I shall be happy to see you when you please; but I fear your engagements, at home and elsewhere, will prevent you.

I am ever yours,
A. R. BOWES.

LETTER XIV.

From the same to the same.

PAUL'S WALDEN, May 30, 1782.

I am extremely sorry that, in consequence of my banker's conduct, you found it necessary to send your servant to PAUL'S WALDEN. That trouble might have been spared you, if my banker had shown you a letter, which I naturally concluded you would see, and which I wrote to him last Tuesday, mentioning, that as my efforts hitherto had failed, I should set off to-morrow for the North, and return with all the speed I could, and bring the money for which you were my security. I hope you are sensible that no man can be more anxious than I am to prevent any inconvenience that you may be apprehensive of feeling; for whatever injuries, whatever gross ingratitude, I may have PRIVATELY met with from an individual, to whom I had unwarily and unworthily pledged my honour and fortune, I shall never exclaim against

those injuries; I shall not return them with a mur-
mur till my engagements are fulfilled, and till I
find a favourable opportunity to make one just and
most expressive requital.

I am surprised at my banker's insolence in writing to you in such a strain, after he knew how
essential, in this affair, your interest was to my
satisfaction. No specious excuse can sufficiently
varnish his conduct, nothing less than the expiring
WEAKNESS of his bank could STRONGLY apologize
for his behaviour. I hope you will communicate
to him this letter of,

Your most faithful friend,
A. R. BOWES.

P. S. I have given Deard a letter, with some
money in it, for one of my annuitants, which
I beg you will direct him to deliver this
night. As YOUR FRIEND, J. W. brought
me in one of the most imposing charges for
business pretended to be done at the late
election, I positively refused to pay him:
the consequence of which is, I have been
served with the enclosed; you will, therefore, desire Mr. H----- to put in an appearance directly, as I have materials that I
think will make him appear one of the
greatest scoundrels existing, and do myself
credit as well as save my money.

LETTER XV.

From William Birch, Esq. to ------ -----, Esq.

DEAN STREET, *November* 15, 1782.

SIR,

Having called repeatedly, without the pleasure of seeing you, I am constrained to write to you on the subject of your unanswered draft on Mr. Bowes. I expected to have heard from you, in consequence of our last meeting, and your intention of seeing Mr. Bowes, and settling something satisfactory with him concerning this business. Since I saw you I have met with Mr. Bowes, who promised me to see you, and to put it in a train for payment to my entire satisfaction. I have heard nothing of him since, and have been unsuccessful in my attempt to see him. I must entreat the favour of hearing from, or seeing you, without further delay, as I cannot account to myself the letting the matter rest as it is. The bill of sale being a mere shadow of security, without an assignment of it. I am very desirous of concurring in any reasonable plan of payment and security; but must insist on the one or the other without further loss of time.

I am,

Sir,

Your most obedient and humble servant,

WILLIAM BIRCH.

LETTER XVI.

From A. R. Bowes, Esq. to ----- -----, Esq.

STREATLAM CASTLE, *December* 15, 1782.

I am favoured with a letter from you, directed to PAUL'S WALDEN, and another dated the 29th of November, which, owing to its having travelled to GIBSIDE, and from thence here, was some time longer in reaching me than it otherwise would have been.

I am extremely sorry to find you so very urgent about the money due to Mr. Birch, which I flattered myself would not have been the case, from Mr. Birch's politeness when we last met in London. From the instances of friendship I have hitherto experienced from you, and, above all, from your knowledge of the difficulties attending my present situation, and the consciousness how rigorously I have, in my dealings with you, attended to all honourable affairs, at least as far as I have had it in my power. I was farther confirmed in this hope, from your being sensible that I sent you up £500 at a time when I was obliged to use EVERY method of procuring it. I am, therefore, greatly grieved and hurt to find you have allowed this matter to go such lengths; and sorry I am to add, that my distress for money, and impossibility of raising it, were never so great as at this juncture, having exhausted every resource, and drained my finances to the utmost, to procure between four and five thousand pounds to send to Mr. G-----y, as the only method to prevent an absolute fore-closure of BENWELL estate for half its value.

I therefore must earnestly request that you will contrive to pay Mr. Birch; and if you entertain any apprehensions on your own account, I now have it in my power to give you ample landed secu-rity. I am the more pressing in this request, as I know you are so fortunate as always to have money at command. Could I have raised the sum requisite to discharge Mr. Birch, I should have been in London before this time; but have waited, and am still waiting, merely on that account.

I am,

Your sincere friend, &c.

A. R. BOWES.

P. S. I find no post goes out from hence to-day; but as I shall go to GIBSIDE to-morrow, I shall put this letter in the DURHAM post in my way thence.

LETTER XVII.

From the same to the same.

GIBSIDE, *April* 15, 1783.

A want of money, not a want of health, has detained me here so long; but I propose setting off for town next Tuesday. and on my arrival shall directly wait upon you, to beg your pardon in per-

son, and to convince you that I have not so bad a
heart as you have reason to suppose. I can make
no apology for my ungenerous neglect, but my natural and habitual indolence, which frequently
renders me dilatory and weak in executing those
offices of politeness and friendship to which, however, I flatter myself my heart is never insensible:
an indolence that I fear will more and more stretch
its leaden sceptre over me. My excuse, I own,
is a very awkward and unsatisfactory one; but yet
it will prove that I deem you my friend*. We are
apt to confess our great failings only to friends;
and friends alone are not only apt to forgive those
failings, but to accept them as substitutes for the
performance of duties. I have ten times more personal and landed property than would pay all my
debts; but then money is as yet not to be bor-
rowed, though I am ready to give you, or any body
else, more than ample real security. You will see
by the enclosed letter what I have to pay the 1st
of June. God knows where it is to come from;
but if it is not paid, my whole BENWELL estate will
be absolutely foreclosed for a sum less than half its
value, without a power of redemption.

I am yours sincerely and truly,

A. R. BOWES.

---

* Here is the first trait of his SHAMMING sickness, which practice never forsook him.

J. F.

The native character, and the real conduct of
Bowes have been as well ascertained by these letters as it was possible to be expected, from one
whose very nature formed him to deceive, and to act
with duplicity, even towards his best and his most
confidential friends. He threw into these miserable
compositions, friendship, adulation, abuse, inde-
pendence, distress, success, despair, prosperity,
and adversity, to suit his own immediate designs.

From the year 1778 to 1783 he was scarcely ever
resident in London. By his last letter it is seen,
that although he was the member for Newcastle,
he did not come to town till April. The fact was,
that, as he has told us, he meant to make something of his parliamentary seat; that he aimed at an
Irish peerage, and finding the administration re-
coiled at it, he grew sulky and abusive.

After having given a few parliamentary dinners
to some of the members and his acquaintances, for
I will not call them friends, he gave up his house
in GROSVENOR SQUARE, and took up his residence
at HOTELS. I remember making a third, with him
and the Duke of ------, at the Star and Garter, Pall
Mall, in this year, 1783. As to what he did in
parliament, there can be no trace, his vote being
always silent. He had been fortunate in having
served the OFFICE of SHERIFF just in time to be
chosen, in 1780, a MEMBER for NEWCASTLE; and
it is beyond all question, that he meditated standing for the county at a future time, and had got
some strong interest on his side. He had also

made the purchase of BENWELL estate from the family of SHAFTO; but this could not have distressed him much, as he mortgaged it deeply; and this he contrived to keep to the day of his death, though from that time to this he raised money upon the plea of losing it.

I am endeavouring to give a SUMMARY of his transactions from the year 1778 to 1783, and to bring it into one point of view; as, during all this time, most of his scene of life lay in the country.

He parted with every thing he could in town, sold CHELSEA HOUSE, and took the family plate into his own possession. He raised £30,000 upon annuities. He insured the life of the Countess only for a year or two at most, by which he squandered away vast sums; whereas had he insured upon a permanent system, his policy would have had a value in proportion to its date, and the money, in some way or other, would have been forthcoming to him again; but he dropped his insurances. He directly went down to GIBSIDE, and CUT DOWN THE TIMBER; the neighbours would not buy it; the felled timber lay upon his hands. He got the nomination of SHERIFF; he opened early his canvass for NEWCASTLE; he entertained the heads of that town at GIBSIDE; he kept an open house; his dinners were good, and his table enriched by massive plate; but there was always a smack of mean splendour about him, as he did not purchase one single new carriage, and his coach horses, originally of high value, were never seen in good

condition.   He took a chaplain into his house, and
had always somebody about him whom he made a
BUT of,

The expences he incurred by his SHRIEVALTY,
by his ELECTION, and HORSE-RACING, by his IN-
SURANCES, and the purchase of BENWELL, kept
him in a constant distress for money; and at the
very time when he wrote this adulatory letter to
his friend, that he never should be happy till he
was out of debt and had some to the good, he
went upon the turf and into an election.   This was
literally the letter of a hypocrite.   He promised
his friend that he would not shew his teeth to his
banker till he could bite; and yet he is seen to
continue him on, and vilify him still.   He got as
much from his banker as he could, and when he
could get no more, he abused the banker and ca-
joled the friend.   He sold the friend his estate
CHEAP; but by his friend being obliged to pay Mr.
Birch, the bargain was all on his side, where it
rested.

He was tremblingly alive for the fate of the
Countess, and watched all her movements like an
ARGUS.   She was delivered of a son, and his anxi-
ety for a time suspended.   When he remained at
GIBSIDE, he avoided his LONDON creditors; but
the time was now approaching, that the creditors'
bills at the election would naturally drive him from
GIBSIDE to LONDON or PAUL'S WALDEN.   Indeed
I have often wondered that he was seen at NEW-
CASTLE two months after his election.   He came

up in April, as his letter tells us, 1783, and there commences his delinquency with his CHIEF agent in the election.

He brought in his company, from the North, Mr. and Mrs. H-----, a worthy and respectable couple. I have reasoned with myself, how it should have happened that two such characters should have been found to be inmates in his house, and so far from their home; and I explained it by supposing, that it was their compassion for the fallen Countess which induced them to forego their own comfort for hers. These two, with the young child, and a nurse of Bowes's, not the Countess's, formed the society of Bowes and the Countess at PAUL'S WALDEN, into which I was twice this year professionally called. Till he could find out a house in town, he made LONDON his visits, and PAUL'S WALDEN his home. The chaplain, Mr. M-----, was gone; and another, Mr. P----- S-----, had left him, after remaining with him about six months. He gave me, as a cause, a strong confirmation of the real character of Bowes.

One cold stormy night Bowes watched a servant maid to her bed, who had resisted all his temptations ; she was the wife of one of his men servants, but Bowes did not, or would not, know this. He saw no light in the man's room. By the help of a ladder he saw them together in the maid's chamber. As soon as the light was put out, he thundered at the door, and turned them out of the house. They took shelter in the lodge. He finding, the next morning, that they had been received by the porter there, turned him away too. The Rev. Mr. S----- was ill, when Bowes visited him at his bed side, and told him all this. And did you do so, said Mr. S-----, YOU who would have ruined her yourself, as you have almost all who come in your way? You shall not turn me out, I will be gone directly. Bowes would not let him have his things till he brought a constable.

I met Bowes in COCKSPUR STREET, towards the autumn, when he went into a JEWELLER's, and purchased some TRINKETS for females, to the amount of forty guineas. He pressed me to come down to PAUL's WALDEN, as he said, to inoculate his child. He had got a new MAN COOK, of Mr. Birch's recommendation; and he was feasting away, giving entertainments to the neighbours, much beyond the necessary stile. Amongst others, there was a most beautiful young woman, one of his farmers' daughters, at dinner, and for whom these TRINKETS were intended. Her mother and sister came after dinner, and they all drank tea with the Countess.

When the company was gone, Bowes asked me to walk out with him; he took me to the farm house, and 'peeped into the window, where they were all sitting, and preparing for bed. Every thing, in their innocent custom, was undoing. The dog barked, and I returned and left him there, where he was for a long while. He told me, there was no danger from the dog, as he had made the farmer tye him up, because, as he said, he had been caught killing some of his own sheep, and that he went thus to the window almost every night. In a week after my return to London he sent for me in haste, as he had met with an accident. The farmer, finding that his dog barked thus every night, suspected thieves, and determined to let him loose; and the dog revenged himself upon Bowes in one of these excursions, fastened upon his leg, and bit it severely.

· The Countess, whom I had not seen for some time before these visits, appeared wonderfully ALTERED and DEJECTED. She was pale and nervous, and her under jaw constantly moved from side to side. If she said any thing, she looked at him first. If she was asked to drink a glass of wine, she took his intelligence before she answered. She sat but a short time at dinner, and then was out of my sight. I did get one morning's walk with her and Mr. Harrison into the once beautiful pleasure garden, where, in spite of the ruinous state of it, much was left for admiration; because the taste which gave it a creation was not as yet totally obliterated. The Countess pointed out to us the concern she had formerly taken in the shrubs, the flower beds, the lawns, the alcoves, and the walks of this most delectable recess. She even pointed out the assistance her own hand had lent to individual articles. In observing her during her conversation, the agitation of her mind was apparent by its action on her mouth. She would look for some time, hesitate, and then her under jaw would act in that convulsive manner, which absolutely explained her state of melancholy remembrance beyond all other proofs abstracted knowledge could confirm, or technical teachers could demonstrate.

One morning whilst I was there, a gentleman was seen riding down the lawn, of whom Bowes told me the following story. Oh! says he, it is R----- B-----. I never expected he would come here again after what passed a fortnight ago. He is a SPUNGER, says Bowes, and comes for my DINNERS and my CLARET. I gave the hint to the rest of the company, and we made him DEAD DRUNK. I put him into an arm chair, had his boots taken off, filled them full of water, put a table cloth round him tucked in at the collar, as barbers do when they shave. I put him on a night cap, placed a table before him with a looking glass, floured his face all over with a kitchen drudger, left candles burning, and we all went to bed. He awoke about five in the morning, before the lights were out; he appeared at a loss to know how this could have happened. His consternation being over, he began to dress to go home. He saw his boots ready to his hand; he flounced his leg into the first, but emptied the water out of the second. In this state he put them on, let himself out, went to the stable, saddled his horse, and went home: and, I dare say, he would not have the smallest objection to be served the very same to-night again. Bowes could scarcely finish his story before the stranger rode up to us: Bowes asked him to dinner, which he of course accepted; but he was very shy that day.

This spunger, as Bowes called him, was an insurance broker in London, and a farmer near Paul's Walden.   Nobody scarcely ever saw the inside of his house.

Bowes, after leaving the former house, took another in Grosvenor Square, ready furnished, of Mr. Windham.   And I am now about to give an important part of his life, that marks him to be of that savage, violent, unfeeling, and lawless nature which may be searched for in the history of man, without any one being able to find its parallel.   It is not one crime, but the continued series of crimes, which compose his character,

Indifferent now about his ambitious concerns, certain that he should never be returned again for Newcastle, he took to study the art of tormenting the trustees and guardians of Lord Strathmore's children, and of getting the two eldest daughters into his possession.   In executing this, he made the Countess his instrument; and if his character, as well as her's, had not been known, every body can tell how strong a ground it is, that the mother shall see her children, and the children their mother.   All of a sudden he appeared to be so tender, so alarmed about the decay of the Countess's health, and the inward pinings, pangs, and sufferings of her peace of mind, that he actually succeeded in getting one of the daughters into his possession, and the other had a very narrow escape.

I will expose this unnatural subject, by a letter

from the unfortunate Countess, whom I do not otherwise implicate in the transaction, than as one under the dominion of Bowes; but still recollecting that she never cared about her children, till he or she were now moved to it. But be that as it may, I feel with human nature in common, that the impulse of a mother to see her children, and of the children to see the mother, is so strong, that nothing but the most abandoned characters can afford the law a point, pretence, or justification, to make any obstruction to its way.

Before I begin this enquiry, I have but a few observations to make, and there is no question about the facts which I am about to bring. I will introduce them with a letter written by the Countess, at the same time I know it was dictated by Bowes, as every part of this transaction is; and perhaps a more deep plot, as referable to domestic life, a more gross imposition on the agents of the law, both counsel and attornies, and a more cruel attack against the morals of youth dependant upon parental authority, were never attempted. The wonder is, how this character escaped those whose duty it was to impugn it.

The guardians of the two young ladies, MARIA JANE and ANNA MARIA, permitted the Countess to see her daughters, but enjoined them to return at night. The Countess had sent a note the day before to Mrs. Carlisle and Este, in Queen Square, on the 21st of May, acquainting them, she should send for Lady Anna Maria the next morning to spend the day with her, that she may have her company before she went on her journey to BATH, as she proposed to do. Accordingly she sent for her on the morning of the 22d of May, 1784, by Mr. and Mrs. Reynett, the clergyman and his wife who resided in the house of Bowes; and instead of Lady Anna Maria returning on the evening of that day, the letter I am just about to give, written by the Countess, was brought by Mr. and Mrs. Reynett, and delivered to Mrs. Carlisle. Mr. and Mrs. Reynett also gave Mrs. Carlisle to understand, that Bowes, the Countess, and Lady Anna Maria, were gone from Grosvenor Square, in a Hackney Coach, they knew not where. Mrs. Carlisle, alarmed at this intelligence, called several times, both that night and the following day. She received the same answer each time, and could get no tidings of Lady Anna Maria, from Mr. and Mrs. Reynett, nor from the servants left in the house, nor did she again return to the school, at least for some time, I believe in February, 1785.

Here follows the letter from Lady Mary Eleanor Bowes Strathmore to Mrs. Este and Carlisle, Queen Square.

GROSVENOR SQUARE, *May* 22, 1784.

LADIES,

I take this method to acquaint you, that in compliance with Lady Anna Maria's affectionate and dutiful request of spending the ensuing holidays with me, I have gratified our mutual wishes, by

taking her into my possession, as the only means
to make myself some recompence for what I have
endured for several years from Mr. L----n's constantly refusing me the company of my children
in such a manner as humanity and propriety seem
to demand.

I should not have taken this step before the appointed day of breaking up, had I not concluded,
that if I waited till then I should be prevented, as
I have hitherto frequently been, by your adhering
to Mr. L----n's orders; which, however, I doubt
not, were highly repugnant to your own wishes,
and very disconsonant * * * * * * * * * to those
sentiments of duty towards a parent, which I am
convinced you would otherwise have been anxious
to instil into the minds of your PUPILS*, and my
daughters.

   I am,
     Ladies,
       Your most obedient humble servant,
       M. E. Bowes Strathmore.

So much for the letter written by Bowes for the
Countess; the very idiom, and the stile altogether,
prove the dictation beyond all question.

It ought to be observed, that both the ladies
were under the protection of the guardians, by an
order of the Court of Chancery. But this was but

---

 * Pupils is Bowes's, not a lady's expression.
             J. F.

half of the deep laid plot. Lady Maria Jane, the
eldest, having left school, resided with her aunt,
Lady A---- S-----, of Harley Street; and the Countess sent Lady A---- S----- also a written request,
that Lady Maria Jane should pay her a visit pre-
vions to her intended journey to BATH. Lady
Maria Jane accordingly went on the 22d of May
also, accompanied, at the request of Lady Maria,
by Mrs. O----, the sister of Lady A---- S-----'s late
husband, when they were shewn into a drawing
room, and received by Mrs. Reynett, and in a few
minutes the Countess came in; and Lady Maria
having told Mrs. O-----, as they went up Grosvenor
Square, that she saw her sister, Lady Anna Maria,
at a window up stairs, Mrs. O----- asked the Countess if Lady Anna Maria was there, when the
Countess acknowledged that she was.

In about a quarter of an hour the Countess desired Lady Maria Jane to walk into the next room
with her, that she may shew her a letter which
she had received from her son, Lord Strathmore:
the Countess went out accordingly, followed by
Lady Maria Jane; Mrs. O----- was left behind,
with Mrs. Reynett and a gentleman, in the room.
Mrs. O----- thinking she had waited long enough,
and growing rather uneasy at her not returning,
rung the bell, and desired the servant to tell Lady
Maria Jane that she was going, and desired her to
come to her. The servant returned, and said that
she was coming presently. Mrs. O----- waited a
short time, and then rung again, and sent the same
message by the servant, but received no answer to

her request. Mrs. O----- then solicited Mrs. Rey-
net to tell Lady Maria that she waited for her.
Mrs. Reynett accordingly went out, and returned
and said to Mrs. O-----, that she dared not go into
the room; upon which Mrs. O----- requested her
to shew her the room, and she would go in herself.
Mrs. Reynett then shewed Mrs. O----- to the Countess's dressing room, which opened upon the back
stairs. Mrs. O----- endeavoured to open the door,
but found it fastened. She then returned into the
drawing room, very much agitated; and soon after,
a servant entered, and brought her a letter from the
Countess, which she received, and of which the
following were the contents:---

GROSVENOR SQUARE, *May* 22, 1784.

MADAM,

As you have accompanied Lady Maria upon the
present, as well as a former occasion, on both of
which I strenuously requested to see my daughter
BY HERSELF, I conclude that you have some written order for that purpose from a majority of her
guardians: if thus authorized, I should not chuse
to interfere, in regard to her returning with you to-
day; but if you cannot produce any such sanction,
you will, I hope, excuse my detaining her till, by
representing my case, and laying my grievances
before my Lord Chancellor, I shall be honoured
with his Lordship's commands.

However inhuman may be the BEHAVIOUR I have
experienced from those who never paid the slight-

est attention to my feelings as a mother, and whose professed regard for my children ought to have taught them a very different lesson; yet I hope you will be so obliging as believe, that nothing can be further from my wishes than to treat you with the most distant degree of impoliteness, especially in my own house; but that goodness of heart which I have the pleasure to know you possess, will, I doubt not, fully excuse the liberty I now take, and lead you to sympathize in the sufferings of a parent, whose children have, for many years, been entirely secluded from her sight, an affliction which, though you have never been so unfortunate as to experience, yet you may easily conceive the severity of; and from your own sensations upon inferior occasions, will form a just idea how impossible it must be even to exist under such cruel and unnatural controul.

I am,

Madam,

Your most obedient and humble servant,

M. E. BOWES STRATHMORE.

Mrs. O----- having read the letter, immediately called for her own servant, and directed him to carry it to his master, wherever he was, and to tell him that she wished him to come to her immediately. Mrs. O----- then told Mrs. Reynett that she would stay till Lady Maria was delivered to her; that Lady Maria was entrusted to her by Lady A---- S-----, who had the charge of her from the guardians; and that she knew that the Countess and Mr. Bowes dared not to detain Lady

Maria from her. And Mrs. O---- then requested Mrs. Reynett to bring Lady Maria to her. She told her, that she did not see any thing of them, and did not know where they were gone. Mrs. O----- then desired to speak to her own coachman, meaning to ask him if he had seen any carriage go from the door; but the servant returned for answer, that he could not find the coachman. Mrs. O----- then returned to the door of the Countess's dressing room, which she found was open; but upon her endeavouring to go in, it was shut against her by some person on the inside; and Mrs. O----- HEARING LADY MARIA SCREAM, she immediately cried out to her, as loud as she was able, MARIA, I WILL NOT QUIT THE HOUSE TILL YOU COME TO ME.

From that moment Mrs. O----- determined not to lose sight of that door; and accordingly desired Mrs. Reynett to procure her a chair, and she would sit down by that door on the back stairs. She did so, and sat herself down on the steps of stairs. Mrs. O----- soon after walked to the great stairs, and Lady Maria came to her, led by a gentleman, without whose interference she would have been a VICTIM. Lady Maria and Mrs. O----- poured their thanks on him, and hastened immediately down the stairs, and out of the house; congratulating herself that she was out of a detestable house, into which she would never enter again; and finding that her chariot was gone, they went immediately to the house of a lady in Lower Grosvenor Street. Lady Maria informed Mrs. O-----, that during the time she was so detained from Mrs.

O-----, Bowes and the Countess, in the most ear-
nest manner possible, endeavoured to persuade
her to withdraw herself from the care of her guardians, and to reside with them.   Lady Maria Jane
was then sixteen years of age,

Application was made to the Chancellor by the
guardians on the 26th, praying to have the person
of Lady Anna Maria delivered over to them.   But
it was too late; as Bowes, who had every thing-
ready for his journey, on the same day he got the
two ladies into his power, absolutely set out that
evening, NOT TO BATH, BUT TO PARIS, and carried
Lady Anna Maria away with him.   The next letter
will prove where he was,

The stile of this adventurer, to the same friend
he wrote the series of former letters, will be very
different.   He then wrote to him to assist and get
money;   he then pleaded poverty, and abused
bankers; but he now aims to intrigue.   If he deceived all other men, why should one be left as an
exception?   I ought to say that Mr. Scott is the
eminent pleader in the Court of Chancery, of that
name; and that Doctor Scott is the physician who
was called in at Bowes's duel.

The following letter was received the 7th of June,
1784; at what time it was put into the post at Paris I cannot say.

LETTER XVIII.

From A. R. Bowes, Esq. to his former Corresponr
dent.

I have only time to say, as the post is going out,
that I have received your letter; but not one word
from Mr. Scott, which disappoints me very much.
Pray send me my letters directed to myself, and I
am in great distress for my red book. The paper
Reynett mentions SHALL be destroyed; therefore
tell him to stick to that he said to Mr. Scott. Tell
Doctor and Mrs. Scott that I will meet them in any
part of France.

I am, &c.

A. R. BOWES

P. S. Mr. Hunter might be a powerful witness
 in Lady Strathmore's favour. I wonder
 you will not send me the letters that are in
 Grosvenor Square. Give Reynett my di-
 rections; tell him to send them to me on
 their arrival in London.

Wednesday Morning.

Post mark, Paris, 1st June, 1784.

LETTER XIX.

From the same to the same.

ₙ   PARIS, *June* 13, 1784.]

I have this instant 'received your very satisfactory letter,[1] for which the ladies' and myself join
in sincerely thanking you. If I had wanted to pe-
tition the Chancellor on the late conduct of the
guardians, I am perfectly well satisfied that the
same diabolical and unfair artifices would have
been successfully practised upon Lady Anna Maria that have deprived Lady Strathmore for ever, I
believe, of the company of her eldest daughter.
Besides, his lordship has been applied to upon two
former occasions, without giving redress; though
no circumstances could be stronger than those
brought against Mr. L-----. The other guardian I
consider merely as a tool, and Mr. O----- the com-
mander in chief. I am now extremely sorry that I
did not turn Mrs. O----- out of the house, and detain Lady Maria. However, I will make J-----
O----- pay for his insolence the first moment I meet
him, let my friends think what they may of the
PRUDENCE of such a step. I am sure your kindness upon examination will do Lady Strathmore
essential service; but Reynett is a blundering poor
fellow, that would do all in his power to serve us,
but has no head. However, there is one good thing,
which is, that he has been always kept in the dark
in every essential that concerned Lady Strathmore's
children, and his wife equally so. It will be,

therefore, prudent, lest they should be examined,
for you to be as little communicative to them as
possible; for if they say any thing, they will likely
say too much. All the service they can do us
will be merely to prove Lady Strathmore's state of
health and mind, which they can perfectly well do,
by just giving the account, UNADORNED, of what
passed from day to day since Mr. Hunter's late
attendance. Mr. Hunter would be a very useful
assistant in this business, if a Scotchman would
speak the truth against the wishes of those of his
own kingdom. He told me two days ago, before
I left town, that Lady Strathmore's disorder was
entirely occasioned by the agitation of mind she
underwent from the cruel absence of her children,
and seemed to wish me to enter into the subject,
which, no doubt, I waved, from the determination
I had taken, and from the thorough knowledge I
have that our views are often destroyed by being
too communicative, and confiding too much in
those who have no interest in being our friends;
or if they have, can only feel it with an inferior degree, and consequently with less precaution. I am
happy in being confident that Mr. Scott's abilities,
zeal, and knowledge of Lady Strathmore's oppres-
sions, will go hand in hand to counteract those insidious plans which have been formed for her destruction. Mr. Lee, too, I am sure, will be a sincere and able advocate. As the post is just going
out, I can only add, that I have not, in my absence from England, a possibility of paying Ran-
dell's money, as really I have but a few hundred
pounds in Child's hands, and that in bills not due

for two months to come. However, I should hope
that Mr. Goostrey would obtain for me so small a
sum upon so ample a security; and as the demand
is pressing, I am willing to pay every premium that
comes under his approbation, in case money is
not to be obtained upon fair terms. Pray when do
you go to the North? Ridley Hall is a charming
spot.

I am truly yours,

A. R. Bowes.

P. S. Pray get Mr. Scott to write to Lady
Strathmore.

LETTER XX.

From the same to the same.

Paris, July 26, 1784.

The number of letters Lady Strathmore and myself have written .to Mr. Scott, without the satisfaction of even the smallest reply, renders us both
extremely unhappy; and the more so, as I am convinced that no good reason, if any is proposed to
be offered, can be alledged for the cruel suspence
we have been kept in for two months past. Indeed
your few favours contained so little relative to the
great object of Lady Strathmore's happiness, that
they gave us not many degrees more comfort than
Mr. Scott's unaccountable and unexpected silence.
Whatever may be the event or the determination of
the Chancellor, respecting Lady Strathmore's

children, I am resolved to return to England immediately after it; though I am equally resolved
to permit Lady S----- and her daughter to do exactly as their own wishes may happen to dictate.
They wish, I believe, to remain in their present
asylum. I beg you will have a full account of the
trial published in ALL the PAPERS the very day it
is over. Whatever may be decided in obedience
to the laws of England, I am certain that every
feeling and IMPARTIAL mind will acquit Lady S----,
and will, all circumstances considered, do me that
justice which I think my conduct towards Lady
S----- and her children deserves. Pray have constant paragraphs inserted relative to Mr. L-----'s
conduct. I will be answerable for them ALL; and
Mr. P----- will take care of them, if you say they
were intended for to serve me.

I am truly and sincerely yours,

A. R. BOWES.

LETTER XXI.

From the same to the same.

PARIS, August 9, 1784.

As the post is just going out, I have only a
single moment to thank you for your obliging letter
of the 3d instant, and to assure you, that I shall
meet the rigour of the law, however far it may be
extended, with great satisfaction, if the impartial
part of the world do not disapprove of the step I
have taken, and that you should meet with no in-

convenience on my account. , Lady Strathmore and myself have written eleven different letters to Mr. Scott since we left England, and all of them put in the post by me. We have never received a letter from him but one while at Calais.

The guardians, through Lord Caermarthen, have made an application to the court of France to have the young lady given up. I took care to have timely information; and shall, I hope, prevent their success. It was cruel that my friends in England were not more upon their guard. They represent the child as taken off under thirteen years of age, for the purpose of getting her married to some improper person, UNKNOWN TO THEM. I hope you will set off for this place the moment your trial is at an end. I can add no more than that

I am ever yours,

A, R, BOWES.

P. S. Pray direct for me in my own proper name, unless you think your letters will be stopped.

LETTER XXII.

From the same to the same.

PARIS, *August* 30, 1784.

The same date this letter bears will, I hope, convey to you one written to inform you that I shall set off from hence to Calais to-morrow, in

order to meet you there; and this is merely written to you as a duplicate, because I am suspicious
that a number of my letters to different people
have been interrupted; but in particular those I
have sent to Mr. Goostrey and Mr. Scott: fourteen to the latter, and three to the former, without
receiving a single reply.

I am very truly yours,

A. R. BOWES.

LETTER XXIII.

From the same to the same.

PARIS, *August* 30, 1784.

------,

I am favoured with both your letters, containing,
in part, what happened in the Court of Chancery.
I lament most exceedingly that I have been the
involuntary cause of the troubles you have lately
experienced, and are still likely to sustain, as far
as I can judge by your own representation. However I cannot conceive how you are thought cul-
pable, except it was from your being the entire
author of preventing Lady Strathmore from gratifying her feelings, when I think, in regard to her
eldest daughter, an exertion of them might have
been expected, and I will venture to add, ought
not to have been left short. As to our immediate
return, no man ever took greater pains than I have
done to convince Lady S—— and her daughter of
the propriety of that step. But it is not in my

power to succeed, without extracting from their minds every dread of what may follow, by the death of my wife, and equally her daughter, their affections are so much interwoven. At all events, however, you must not suffer for me. Every experiment was tried to soften the conduct of Mr. L---n. You have neglected me much, by not keeping your promise of visiting me. I shall set out from hence to Calais early to-morrow morning. By your meeting us, you will have an opportunity of stating matters in their true colours to both the ladies. As to myself, I am ready to attend the wishes of the Chancellor, and to confess I assisted Lady S----- in the execution of this affair. Our greatest astonishment is at Mr. Scott's total silence since we left Calais, though we have written no less than fourteen letters to him since our arrival here. Pray forward the inclosed to him, and write to him yourself, to desire that he will send a letter to Lady Strathmore, under cover to you at Calais, for Lady S-----. It may then, perhaps, arrive safe. Bring my writing box. Tell Reynett to forward letters to me. I beg he may not know a word about our intended meeting at Calais. I know him well.

I am very truly yours,
A. R. Bowes.

LETTER XXIV.

From the same to the same.

PARIS, *August* 31, 1784.

As I flatter myself my letter of yesterday's date will bring you to Calais nearly as soon as this arrives there, I therefore take the liberty of requesting that you will immediately extend your journey to Lisle, where you will find me at the Hotel de Bourbon, sur la Grand Place. On many accounts it is better we should meet there; and I should have conveyed that wish to you in my last letter, but in case they should have been interrupted, I thought this precaution expedient.

I am very truly yours,

A. R. BOWES.

P. S. I wish you to tell Dessin you are going to Paris, and every person you meet at Calais, the reason is obvious.

LETTER XXV.

From the same, at Paris, to the same, at Calais.

PARIS, *September* 4, 1784.

------,

Lest the letter I wrote to you, two days ago, to Calais should not get safe to your hands, I think it proper to repeat, that I shall be much disappointed if I should not find you there. I did not set off according to my promise in my last letters, because I found, upon calculating the time, it was impossible for my first letter to reach you so soon as I had imagined.

I am very truly yours,

A. R. Bowes.

P. S. I shall be at the Hotel de Bourbon, at Lisle, a la Grande Place.

LETTER XXVI.

From the same to the same.

Paris, *September* 12, 1784.

------,

I have been confined to my bed with a painful and violent rheumatic fever ever since the evening preceding the day which I had destined to set off to meet you; however, though far from being in a proper situation to undertake a journey, I am determined to quit this place to-morrow, and shall be with you as expeditiously as my disorder will admit. I do assure you I have felt extreme distress at the apprehension that you may have been waiting, as

I am very truly yours,

A. R. Bowes.

LETTER XXVII.

From the same to the same.

LISLE, *September* 16, 1784.

I have for some time suspected that Dame Fortune had forgotten her old connection, and left me upon the barren shore to shift for myself; but that suspicion is no longer one, it is realized by the mortification I have met in not finding you here. However, as you are sufficiently acquainted with my unhappy feelings upon trifling occasions, I submit to you what must be my sensations when a suspension of that intelligence still subsists, which, by the action of the mind on the body, has almost torn me from this earth.

The inclosed letter has been here several days; and was found by myself at the bottom of a drawer in the bar, along with yours of the 13th, neither of which would the sagacity of the people here have allowed me, had it not been for my own researches, after being repeatedly told there was no letter for me, and that they did not recollect any gentleman of your name being here. I shall shortly say that my delay was occasioned by what the physicians termed the gout in the head, and to such a degree, that my leaving Paris so soon was deemed madness. I am, notwithstanding, wonderfully better; and if Mr. Scott's letter had come to my hands, and contained any thing that would induce Lady S----- and her daughter to go quietly

to England, it would, I am convinced, be of more
real benefit to me than all the gout cordials the
whole faculty ever prescribed.   If it is not full and
decisive, I may as well put a dagger in their breasts
as use that compulsion which upon some occasions
I should think proper and prudent.   Your attendance at Calais, in case Mr. Scott should be in
the least doubtful relative to Lady Strathmore's
hopes, will be absolutely necessary; as soon as
this letter is m the post I shall set off for that place,
and shall get there on Thursday evening.   To press
you to return to me then after the trouble you have
already had, is more than I can venture to do,
however strong my wishes are.   Direct to me at
Dessins.   But if Mr. Scott has REALLY written to
me before, his letter may be again intercepted, and
it may therefore be imprudent to direct to me;
in that case direct it, under cover, to Mr. Alexan-
der Pope, at Dessins, at Calais, if you should not
happen to be the messenger yourself.

Would it be possible now for me to borrow
£17,000 upon my Benwell estate immediately?   It
is £1300 per annum, and I will give a premium of
£500.   I must get clear of all little demands.

   Adieu!

     Yours ever,

       A. R. BOWES.

LETTER XXVIII.

From the same to the same.

CALAIS, *September* 19, 1784.

A------,

I shall wait here till I see or hear from you, with that impatience which naturally arises from my situation, and the perpetual agonies of distress that attends Lady Strathmore and her daughter, from the dread of being parted from each other. My letter to you from Lisle, of the 16th instant, I hope you have received before this time. I have just taken a letter out of Dessin's office, which I wrote to you from Lisle, in order to take the chance of its catching you here; but your friend Strode tells me that Newmarket could not do without you.

I am very truly yours,

A. R. BOWES.

At length Bowes was brought back, with the Countess and Lady Anna Maria, by his friend.

Bowes had so worked upon the Countess as to make her affect not to see his friend for two days after his arrival; and when he saw her she was obliged to pretend to faint, although it was the wish of her heart to come over to England. Bowes made the Countess write his friend a letter, complaining of his barbarity in obliging her to come

over. His friend was almost disposed to return
the second time without her and Lady Anna Maria, and take all consequences with the Lord Chan
cellor.

Fearful that I might be thought to have already
trespassed too much upon the patience of the
reader, in the narrative of this violent measure of
Bowes's, I shall give my reason why I was thus
particular in exposing those letters from him to
the extent which they are seen : it was to mark
his character in a more convincing and striking
manner than by any other means it could possibly
be disclosed.

He dwells on the necessity there was for the
daughter's being with the Countess, to preserve her
very existence. He avows her bad state of health,
and attributes it to the cruel treatment of the guardians. He is all submission to the will of the
Countess. He writes in every letter to his friend,
about the silence of Mr. Scott, on purposes of the
first importance to his designs. For he would have
used any letter from that gentleman, as a means of
vindicating himself both in PARIS and in LONDON.
Had he but got a letter, the English ambassador,
would have been influenced by it, and the court of
France would have considered the case as a common question of law. A letter was thus called for
also, to answer the purpose of deceiving the very
friend with whom he corresponded ; for as he has
avowed in one of his letters, how he deceived Reynett, so would he deal with every body else. He

aimed to inspire his friend with confidence, **by** shewing how much he possessed the confidence **of** Mr. Scott; and this sort of dealing was the practice of his life.

I do believe that both Mr. Scott and Mr. Lee were persuaded that the Countess was the mover of this transaction, from affection; that her ill health was owing to her being deprived of the comfort of her children; and that Bowes was acting the part of a benevolent husband, by thus waiting upon her wishes; for when the cause was argued, both these high and humane characters pleaded with their eyes brimful of tears.

It must not be dissembled that, from what will appear hereafter in his life, I am convinced that the reason he assigned, which was sickness, for not meeting his friend on the first appointment at LISLE, by which his friend was obliged to return without him, and thereby subject himself to the censure of the Court of Chancery, was all a FICTION. His letters either are sincere or hypocritical; if they be sincere, and if the tenor of his heart be in unison with them, if the Countess saw them, and could vouch for the truth of their statement, Bowes then might have passed, in this transaction, only as a violent and abrupt man, but not as a wicked one. But if the whole be falsehood and dissimulation, a pretence of virtue for the success of vice, if he wanted to get the two ladies into his possession, he then has proved himself to be a most consummate hypocrite. In that view, these

letters may be read as a masterpiece of villainy;
not as we see such of this description in CLARISSA,
but as realized and connected with a history,
which will not fail hereafter to excite the strongest
movements of sympathy.

The real intention will soon be unfolded. Shortly
will be seen the art which, Bowes has employed,
and the use to which he has applied those strong
and social ties which unite and bind the happiness
of our existence, the mutual affections of parent
and child towards each other: and shortly we
shall see that the hypocrite, under the shield of
the highest qualities of virtue, commits his foul
deeds, and vainly thinks himself safe from the eye
and vengeance of the world. If example be intended to effect anything for the better guarding
of innocence against the arts of a villain, this Life
of Bowes may afford some instruction; as who can
say, after this, that fictitious characters, as they
are drawn by the novelist, can be ever over-
strained.

All the delight of the fond heart of a woman of
fashion, possessing an immense fortune, high education, and strong propensities for figuring in the
BEAU MONDE, and for displaying the resistless or-
namental appendages of exalted rank, was by
Bowes suppressed. The rich, the gay, and fa-
shionable equipage, the well-disciplined and flirt-
ing fan, the proud and nodding plumage, the bril-
liant and superb diamonds, the conspicuous opera
box, the love-exciting dance, the soft and extatic

endearments of the Italian song, which was better
tasted by the Countess than most ladies, from her
perfect knowledge of the language and of music,
were all compressed, and totally obliterated. Her
person, accustomed only to distress and confinement, found no alleviation of the bitterest sorrow.
Mind and body jointly submitted to receive the
pressure which Bowes, like a MANGLE, daily rolled
upon them, and both were grievously collapsed.

At the time when the Countess surrendered her
liberty to Bowes, she had, among other high en-
dowments, brought her mind to a taste for poetical
composition. She had composed and printed a
dramatic performance, of five acts, called the
SIEGE OF JERUSALEM; and in the voluptuous trance
which was raised in her mind by the DUEL, she
sported the following VERSES

ON THE NUPTIALS.

Unmov'd, MARIA saw the splendid SUITE
Of rival captives sighing at her feet,
'Till in her cause, his sword young S—n—y drew,
And to revenge, the gallant wooer flew!
Bravest among the brave!—and first to prove,
By death! or conquest! WHO best knew to love'
But pale, and faint, the wounded lover lies,
While more than pity fills MARIA's eyes!
In her soft breast! where passion long had strove,
Resistless sorrow fix'd the reign of LOVE!
" Dear youth," she cries, " we meet no more to part!
" Then take thy honour's due,—my BLEEDING heart!"

      M.

How changed is the present condition of the heart, to be forced to quit the person here described from abhorrence, from fear, from want of even clothes, and from hunger! How mistaken mortals form delusive plans of bliss, how they claim futurity for their own, and how, notwithstanding these prospective dreams beguile the truth, they are not masters of a single moment, nor can they anticipate what may be to-morrow! At the time the Countess escaped, she had not a shilling at her command; no other dress but what she had on; her JEWELS even were forgotten; so inestimable is the value, and so coveting is the magnitude of LIBERTY, that whenever it be seriously contemplated, it absorbs all other subordinate considerations.

I am at the same time free to confess, that there were those who thought the restraint upon the Countess, by her not being permitted to see her children, a hardship; but I am also aware, that they were not well informed of the real state of the family. It was the knowledge of character which made the guardians so strict, and the Court of Chancery so peremptory: and if the case be left to character, a very short period will shew, that a discernment of the difference between a good and a bad one, is one of the most certain guides for wisdom to steer by.

It is now about the beginning of November, 1784, that I am upon the proceedings in the Court of

H

Chancery on this subject, and on the 7th of February, 1785, WITHIN THREE LITTLE MONTHS, THE COUNTESS OF STRATHMORE EXHIBITED ARTICLES OF THE PEACE IN THE COURT OF KING'S BENCH, AGAINST HER HUSBAND, ANDREW ROBINSON BOWES, FOR ILL TREATMENT OF HER PERSON. The Countess desired to have one of the tipstaffs for her protection to her residence, which was granted.

Letter from A. R. Bowes to his friend, upon this occasion.

Though perhaps I have lost your friendship, yet I am clear your good offices will still continue to assist me in the hour of distress. Mr. Harborne promised me two or three days notice in case Lady Strathmore should determine upon the step she has taken. Let me know directly if I am to be arrested to-night, that I may see Mr. Lee and Mr. Scott immediately upon the business.

I am yours, &c.

A. R. BOWES.

4 o'clock.

By this letter to his friend, he is still harping upon Mr. Scott.

A day or two before the Countess appeared in the Court of King's Bench, Bowes dined at Captain Armstrong's, in Percy Street, which gave the Countess the opportunity to elope, by the assistance of Mrs. Morgan, who had lived with the family nearly twelve months, and who was a strong advocate in her favour.

The measure had been for some time meditated on ; but the difficulty was, to find the opportunity. The male servants were dispatched for some pretended purpose or other; he who was appointed to watch her was sent to the stationer's for some book of amusement for the Countess to read, and fill up her time, in the absence of Bowes. Some doors were locked, that it might not be too soon found out that she was gone; and thus they stole out of the house, and got undiscovered into Oxford Street, where they were for a long while obliged to 'wait, there not being any coach upon the stand.

However, they at length got safe into one, and just as they came opposite to Berner's Street, Mrs. Morgan saw Bowes in a Hackney Coach also, driving very fast, with his head out, and without his hat. Providentially he saw them not; but the escape was so narrow, that the Countess, in her low state of health, from the representation upon her mind of the misery which threatened her, if she should be retaken, fell into hysterics, and was with difficulty persuaded that she was safe, and out of his power.

Bowes had been fetched as soon after their escape as possible. His carriage was brought; but when the servant announced to him what had hap-

pened, he ran into Oxford Street, without saying
one word, left his hat and carriage behind him,
took a Hackney Coach, and drove home.

The Countess was conducted, by Mrs. Morgan,
to Mr. Shuter's the barrister, in Cursitor Street;
and an apartment was taken for her in Dyer's
Buildings, where she remained, and where Bowes
at length discovered her, but not till she was under
the protection of the Court.   His bail, I think, was
the Duke of Norfolk, and that respectable lawyer,
John Lee.

Bowes soon resolved upon taking lodgings in the
same street, to be there now and then, and to keep
watch upon her.   He took every step he possibly
could, without infringing the law, to get the Countess again into his possession.

All the foul-weather birds were hovering about his
distressed house in Grosvenor Square; there used
to come, one after the other, such a draggled tail set
as are seen, in wet weather, canvassing about at
elections.   A more pitiable object I never beheld
than Bowes.   His mind was every moment upon
some new device; and although he had more than
a dozen engines at work, I am confident not one of
them knew what the other was about.   One of the
maids of the house was with child by him; and she
was sent away, where he hoped they could not find
her, as this might have been a charge against him
in the Commons.   This was a prize of immense
value, if they could but make their capture, and

carry her into Doctor's Commons. They had found her out, and he must now remove her. He dressed up one of those engines in his employ in the very dress that his friend wore, with whom he had so long corresponded, who took upon him to remove her, and in which he succeeded. The reason why he dressed the man so as to personate his friend, was to induce the Countess's law friends to swear to a wrong person, not caring at all about the use he made of his own friend.

He laid all his plans now over the bottle. He sat up all the night, drinking very hard, and eating high seasoned things, particularly peppered biscuits. The law, both in the Commons and King's Bench, was appealed to. George, the Countess's favourite footman, had carried away, in his own trunk, the Countess's DEED OF TRUST, which he had preserved at the very bottom of it; and notwithstanding Bowes had searched it, yet it escaped him.

Bowes was not aware that this antenuptial DEED was in existence;---this DEED which gave the decisive turn to every thing against him. The Countess, for once, very faithful to herself, deceived him. In Massinger's comedy of " a new Way to pay old Debts," Wellborn gets his writings from Sir Giles Overreach much after the same felicitous and providential manner. Massinger formed his own plot, and consequently, as a punishment for the iniquitous character of Sir Giles, gave it the moral issue, not of accident but of justice. There is a providence in the fall of a sparrow, and this good man and excellent dramatic poet thought so.

I have a letter from this same GEORGE now before me, in which he acknowledges the receipt of ten pounds, to appear for Bowes in the Court of Chancery on the 1st of February, but concealed himself, and kept away. He modestly writes for more money.

Every fool could now overreach him. Within six months of the elopement, though the cause was not definitive, nor the case completely and finally settled, yet within that space of time every intelligent person could discover, from the issue of that trial in the Court of King's Bench, that Bowes no longer would enjoy one single sixpence from the Bowes's property. Castles and rents all melted away like the baseless vision of a dream.

Even the house in Grosvenor Square was surrendered with his last hope. It was a ready furnished house; and Mr. Froggat, Mr. Windham's attorney, gave him permission to leave a service of plate in the house, for which reason he easily gave up the key. This plate, in a chest, was put into a room at the top of the house, and Mr. Froggat took charge of it. This secured the rent, whenever he was called upon to pay it; and this was equally a security to Bowes that his plate had a safe lodgement.

So sudden was her departure, that the Countess

left even all her jewels behind, which Bowes's friend took away·with him, and which Bowes thought were safe FOR HIM in his hands. These he lodged at Child's house, and they were, by that means saved to the family. Their value was not less than £10,000, and which Bowes never forgave.

The Countess, after her elopement, until she had ·obtained, through Mr. Shuter her council, and Mr. Seton of the Adelphi her attorney, this decisive success to her future hope, by the trial in the Court of King's Bench, was left in- a very disconsolate state; there were none to help her in this time of need, save the two gentlemen I have just named: I believe General Lambton did call on her, and made her a present: she was reduced very low indeed: but so soon as this cause succeeded, ‸friends poured in; and new council and new attornies rushed forward upon the opening of this door of Paradise. She was removed to Hart Street, from thence to Bloomsbury Square, had a coach at her command, and·a man of the name of LUCAS, a constable of high respectability, to attend and protect her every where. In short, she was caressed, and had all the freedom which the money they fed her with would permit: whilst those who had first taken up her cause were ungratefully neglected.

Bowes, in this moment of distress, had naturally an EYE to a prison: and his taste for a good dinner, under all his afflictions, led him to the City Coffee

House, on Ludgate Hill, which is within the rules. After a little coquetry with Mr. Froggat, in trying to get the plate out of the house without paying the rent, he at length found the money, and Mr. Froggat gave up the plate to Bowes. It was at the adjustment of this that I dined at the Coffee House with them.

Bowes, who certainly possessed an unsatisfied and restless mind, and who chose just as well to be reduced to a situation for the exercise of the natural bent of his genius for intrigue, had a most fertile harvest open before him. The Doctors' Commons was quite at his service for the reception of the record of all his illegitimate children for these last nine years, and the crop was not unproductive: it was vastly more, perhaps, than the granary of any other man has been found to produce.

Besides these transactions, which were some of them visitings to the mind, not unaccompanied with ideas of unwelcome pleasure, there were others of a more grievous and bitter kind, and in which the most depraved mind could find no repast nor content. The proofs which were exhibited against him in the Commons, of the cases, which consisted in beating, scratching, biting, pinching, whipping, kicking, imprisoning, insulting, provoking, tormenting, mortifying, degrading, tyrannizing, cajoling, deceiving, lying, starving, forcing, compelling, and a new torment, wringing of the heart, were all necessary to engage his attention, to employ his native disposition, and to call upon its utmost exertion, in order to set them aside.

What a singular circumstance it is, that a man should have actually taken so much pains to be at variance with his own, and which is every man's own, real felicity, and even with the tranquillity of others! What a miserable sort of energy! What a state of human depravity, without any common and fair defined motive for such an inducement!

Every epithet above given will find a classification in the catalogue produced and printed, which issued on the part of the Countess from the Commons; but which, if I detailed them, would be offensive in their particulars to the tender and delicate eye of chastity, as in the Commons the proofs must be made out so plain, that the most minute circumstances must appear: the law probes and lays open offences, but the biographer must be permitted to give them a sort of varnish---must so describe bad actions and loose manners as to make them look a little better, and render them, without losing but as small a portion of their essence as possible, acceptable to the public eye.

To these allegations, Bowes had not much to oppose. He, by way of a set off, put the Countess's CONFESSIONS into the hands of his proctor, to make the most of them. But what could they do? The CONFESSIONS contained transactions only before their marriage; treasures which Bowes had provided and preserved IN TERROREM; which

he laid behind his pillow by night, and read them
by scraps, for his purposes, by day, which he had
gotten by heart, and which formed a part of his
travelling equipage to Paris, and every where else;
which he hugged to his bosom, and over which he
brooded with a rancorous rapture.

But still Bowes had a full employment. His
business was to bribe all the servant maids he
could, whom he had despoiled, to silence the
cries of their distressed children, and to keep hunger and ruin out of the way of any honest justification and strong temptation. But in spite of all
this, there were enough who found their way to
Doctors' Commons to answer the Countess's purpose.

When the Countess left Dyer's Buildings, Bowes
gave up his apartments there; but not before he
left there also his representative with the maid
servant. The Countess went from thence into
Hart Street, and soon after into Bloomsbury
Square. Bowes took his stand in lodgings in
Gloucester Street; and here he meditated upon the
last effort he was ever permitted to make upon the
person of the Countess.

Having, both drunk and sober, framed in his
own mind the plan which he meant to carry into
effect, he began to put it into practice. The first
step towards it was TO UNDERMINE LUCAS, the
constable appointed to protect the Countess, and
who resided in the house with her, and was always

in attendance on her. He found out where his wife and family lived: he gratified all their immediate wants: he made himself out an injured man: he produced his credentials, the CONFESSIONS: and he, by time and close attention, soon got the wife and her visitors on his side. " Sure he is a charming man, and 'twas a shame he should be so used; he is as mild and as meek as a lamb, 'and as good and generous as a prince. One of my children was ill---he saw it every day---nursed it---and gave it the medicines himself." By his constancy in persevering, with all the warmth of sincerity, he succeeded in gaming LUCAS over to his purpose.

BOWES having settled every thing with LUCAS, went into the North; and in October he had even appointed the day, the 10th of the next month, for coming to town. I am apt to think that he had another intention by writing the letter which follows to me, besides taking the house, and which he was certain I should not do; it was, that in case his plan had miscarried, he might have been able to say, that he had so long ago determined to be in London on that day, to prove also that he was away, and to put me off my guard.

LETTER.

From A. R. Bowes, Esq. to Jesse Foot, Esq.

STREATLAM' CASTLE, NEAR BARNARD
CASTLE, *October* 13, 1786.

DEAR SIR,

As I have experienced your friendship upon different occasions, I am not at all afraid of still pressing upon it, because your understanding gives me more than an idea of its extent. However, as I I am over a bottle, and have already drank at least one, I shall, without any other apology, request that, in the course of your morning walks, you will find me a little snug house in the neighbourhood of St. James's, UNFURNISHED, and fit for the reception of myself and half a dozen servants IN ALL; with a coach house, and stables for four horses at least. I intended to have been in town before this time; but am now so situated, that I fear I shall not have the pleasure of seeing you before the 10th of next month.

I am,

Dear Sir,

Your very sincere friend and obedient servant,

A. R. BOWES.

Bowes did not certainly come to reside in town before the 10th; but he soon followed the above letter, and came up to Paul's Walden, where he settled his definitive plan. And I recollect perfectly having a note from him of invitation to come down there,, which if I had happened to have obeyed, I most certainly should have returned to town with him on the 10th of November, and been driven off with him and the Countess into the North; and the world would never have been persuaded that I was not in the plot.

Here follows a narrative of this violent measure, faithfully given.

FROM THE GENTLEMAN'S MAGAZINE, DEC. 1786.

NARRATIVE OF THE LATE ATTEMPT ON THE LIBERTY OF LADY STRATHMORE.

Some weeks previous to the day of carrying the conspiracy formed against her into execution, several suspicious persons were seen lurking about her Ladyship's house in Bloomsbury Square; and the same persons were observed frequently to follow her carriage, sometimes in hackney coaches, and sometimes on foot

Her Ladyship was not wholly unapprized of their attendance, nor unapprehensive of their designs; but, to counteract their measures, she took in her weekly pay one Lucas, a constable, to keep a constant eye upon her carriage, whenever she went out, and never to be out of call.

This man, on Friday, the 10th of November, enquired of the coachman, as his custom was, if his lady went out that day? And was answered in the affirmative; and received orders to attend between one and two in the afternoon. About that time her Ladyship had business at Mr. Foster's, in Oxford Street; and, for company, took Mr. Farrer, brother to her solicitor, and her maid, Mrs. Morgan, in the coach with her. In their way they met with no interruption; but they had scarce been five minutes in the house of Mr. Foster before some of those persons came into the shop, who had been marked as above, and were well known to her Ladyship.

Being much alarmed at their appearance, she withdrew to an inner room, and locked the door, requesting Mr. Foster, at the same time, to go privately and procure assistance, to be in readiness for her protection, in case any violence should be offered to her person.

Mr. Foster had scarce left the house, when the constable, whose business it was to watch the motions of his lady, went up and tapped at her room door, and by telling her his name, obtained immediate admittance. Interrogating him as to his business, she was ready to sink when she was told, that her Ladyship was his prisoner; that a warrant had just been put into his hands; that he must do his duty; but that it was rather fortunate for her ladyship, as he would take her before Lord

Mansfield, at Caenwood, who, no doubt, would frustrate all the wicked purposes of her enemies, and take her under his own immediate protection. With this artful tale, in the then state of her mind, she was easily prevailed on to step again into her coach, as Mr. Farrer was permitted to accompany her. The moment she was seated, her servants were all discharged, by a pretended order from her Ladyship, a confederate coachman mounted the box, and a new set of attendants, all armed, surrounded the coach. In this manner they proceeded, without noise or interruption, till they reached Highgate Hill, at the bottom of which stood Mr. Bowes, who, addressing himself to Mr. Farrer, very civilly requested to change places with him, and then seated himself at the right hand of his Lady, who was no longer in doubt as to his design. The coachman was now ordered to proceed, and to quicken his pace.

Mr. Farrer, being now at liberty, made all possible haste to London, and application was made immediately to the Court of King's Bench, in order to effect a rescue. On Monday, the 13th, two of Lord Mansfield's tipstaffs set off for that purpose to the North. In the mean time, Mr. Bowes continued his journey.

At Barnet fresh horses were ready to put to, and a post chaise and four, with some accomplices, were in waiting to attend. Though the windows of the coach were broken, and the lady in the coach appeared in great distress, yet not the least effort was made to interrupt their progress; and it was not till the next day at noon, when a servant of Mr. Bowes's arrived at the Angel Inn, in Doncaster, 195 miles from London, and ordered horses to be ready to put to his master's coach, that we have any account of their further proceedings. In half an hour the coach stopped in the street; and while the horses were changing, Mr. Woodcock, the master of the inn, handed some cakes to Mr. Bowes, which Mr. Bowes presented to the lady; but whether she accepted them or not he could not positively assert. The moment the horses were in harness, they pursued their course northward; and the next notice we have of them was at Branby-Moor, where the lady was shewn into a room, attended by a chambermaid, and guarded by Mr. Bowes, who hastened her return, and seemed all impatience till she was again seated in the coach. At Ferry Bridge she had leave to go into the garden; but Mr. Bowes waited at the door.

What further passed till they arrived at Streatlam Castle, in the principality of Durham, remained a secret till her Ladyship's arrival, on Tuesday, the 21st of November, in the evening, at the house of Messrs. Farrer and Lacy, on Bread Street Hill. The detail she then gave of her sufferings, during the eleven days of absence, was truly pitiable. At the time of taking her away, the confederates were alarmed; that, as they drove along, Mr. Bowes endeavoured to persuade her to sign a paper, to stop proceedings in the ecclesiastical court, and to consent to live under the name and character of his wife, both which she positively refused to do; that he then beat her on the face and body with his clinched fists, that when she endeavoured to cry out, he thrust a handkerchief into her mouth; that, on the most trifling contradiction, while on the road, he beat her with the chain and seals of his watch on the naked breast; and that when provoked by her firmness, he presented a loaded pistol to her head, and threatened her life if she did not instantly sign the paper, but this she was determined never to do.

Being arrived at Streatlam Castle, he then endeavoured to persuade her to take upon her the government of the family, and to act in every respect as his wife, which she still most solemnly refused to do. On which, in a glow of passion, he pulled out a pistol, bid her say her prayers, and, with a trembling hand, presented it at her head. This too failing of effect, he violently beat her, then left her, and she saw no more of him for a whole day; when coming up to her room rather more calm than usual, he asked her, if she was not yet reconciled to a dutiful domestic life? and being answered with some asperity, he flew into a more violent passion than she had ever yet seen him, pulled out the pistol, bid her say her last prayers, she did say her prayers, and then bid him fire!

By this time the whole country began to be alarmed for her, and he for his own safety. He, therefore, in order to cover his escape, and to keep her still in his power, ordered two of his domestics to be dressed so as to personate himself and her Ladyship, and to shew themselves occasionally before the windows, to appease the populace, and to deceive his pursuers. This stratagem had its full effect; the people were quiet while they thought her Ladyship was safe; and the sheriff's officers, who were sent to execute the attachment, actually served it on the wrong persons; while, in the mean time, Bowes took her out by a back way, dragged her between ten and eleven o'clock, in the dark, to a little cottage in the neighbourhood, where they spent the remainder of the night, and where he behaved to her in a manner shocking to the delicacy of civil life, by reiterating his threatenings, and, finding threats in vain, throwing her on the bed and flogging her with rods. On leaving the cottage in the morning, he had her set on horseback behind him, without a pillion, and took her over dismal heaths and trackless wilds covered with snow, till they came to Darlington, to the house of Mr. B------, the attorney, where she was shut up in a dark room, and where she was threatened (a red hot poker being held to her breast) with a mad doctor and strait waistcoat; but all in vain. The hour of deliverance drew near. Here they had been tracked, and here it was no longer safe for Bowes to continue; he therefore set out with her before day, in the same manner that he brought her, taking her over hedges and plowed fields, till, being seen by the husbandmen at work, he was so closely hemmed in, that an old countryman taking hold of his horse's bridle, and Bowes presenting his pistol to frighten him, he was knocked down by a constable that was in

pursuit of him, and felled to the ground with a large
hedge stake.   Seeing him in that situation, her
Ladyship put herself under the protection of the
peace officer, and being on horseback, in a kind of
womanish exultation, bid him farewell, and mend
his life, and so left him weltering in his blood;
while she, with the whole country in her favour,
made the best of her way to London, attended only
by her deliverers, where she arrived safe, as has
already been related.

On Wednesday the 22d, she appeared in the
Court of King's Bench, but the Court being up, no
proceedings could that day be had on her case.

On Thursday the 23d, she was again presented
in Court; and as soon as the Judges were seated,
Mr. Law, her counsel, moved, " That she might
exhibit articles of the peace against her husband,
A. R. Bowes.

The articles were then read, precisely in substance as already recited ; and, being sworn to and
signed, an attachment was immediately granted
against Bowes.

On Friday the 24th, Mr. Chambré, counsel for
Bowes, moved the Court in behalf of his client,
to have the writ for producing him enlarged till the
third day of next term, he giving ample security for
his appearance. This motion was grounded on an affidavit of Bowes, stating, that after the service of the
Habeas Corpus, he had, in compliance proceeded

to bring Lady Strathmore to town, but was unable
to ford the River Dee with safety to her Ladyship
and himself. In consequence of which, he was
returning by a nearer way, when he was met by the
party who were sent to execute the attachment, by
whom he was treated as has been already related.

The Judges Ashurst and Buller informed the
counsel, that his application came too late; that,
had it come sooner, it could not have been complied with, as such a procedure would entirely
destroy the purpose of an attachment; and as an
additional reason, they alledged the late affidavits
received by the Court.

Mr. Law, her Ladyship's counsel, then moved,
" That the affidavit of Bowes might be filed,
that, if any thing was advanced in it which should
be disproved hereafter, an indictment might lie
against him for perjury; the affidavit of Bowes being
in express contradiction to the affidavit of Lady
Strathmore." Mr. Law also obtained a rule to shew
cause against Peacock, Lucas, and Prevost,
Bowes's assistants, as also against Mr. Bourne, his
steward, and Mr. B-------, his attorney; but the
rule, for reasons that are obvious, was not made
absolute.

On Monday the 27th, Bowes was produced in
Court, to answer the articles exhibited against
him by Lady Strathmore as above recited.

Bowes was dressed in a drab-coloured great

coat, a red silk handkerchief about his head; he
was supported by two men, yet nearly bent double
with weakness, in consequence of his wounds; he
frequently appeared on the point of fainting, and
his appearance, on the whole, was the most squalid
and emaciated that can possibly be imagined.

Mr. Mingay, counsel for Lady Strathmore, desired articles might be read, which being complied
with, he observed, that no farther progress could be
made at present, as whatever reply was made, must
be in the form of affidavits.

The manner of apprehending him, as told by his
friends, differs widely from that told by Lady
Strathmore. They say nothing of the cottage;
but that, a few hours before the Habeas Corpus
was served, apprehending an attachment, he took
the Countess of Strathmore with him in a post
chaise, and directed his route northward. Being
pursued by different parties, he was compelled to
alter his course almost perpetually, and, forsaking
the coach road, to take his journey through the
mountains, subject to all the inconveniences stated
by her Ladyship. Leaving the post chaise, he took
the Countess with him on a single horse, and instead of a pillion, was forced to substitute a blanket.
At one period his pursuers were within a mile of
him; being apprized of it, he changed his course,
and travelled back seventeen miles of the way he
had already passed, and proceeded towards Dar-
lingtou. A few miles from that town he was met by
two farmers, one of them declared his suspicions,

but having no warrant, Bowes drew a pistol, and, with violent menaces, threatened them if they interrupted him; a crowd coming up, the pistol was wrested from him and broken; he was pulled from his horse, and in his fall received two violent wounds on the back part of his head with the barrel, which, with the fall, deprived him of all power of further resistance.   Bowes was then taken to the house of Mr. B------- attorney, at Darlington, where, notwithstanding his wounds, he knocked down the farmer that stopped him, and had him kicked out of the house.   A posse of people, however, soon surrounded the house, and an express was sent to M'Manus, and other Bow-street people, then at Carlisle, who broke in upon him, executed the writ, and notwithstanding every stratagem to delay time, conducted him to London, and produced him, as has just been recited.

I am now about to present a letter from Bowes, after his seizing the Countess, before she was rescued from him, and before he was brought up to town in custody.

LETTER.

From A. R. Bowes, Esq. to Jesse Foot, Esq.

STREATLAM CASTLE, (the post mark
date is) *Nóvember* 21, 1786.

[Bowes's date of it is on the 11th of November.]

MY DEAR SIR,

I was much mortified at not MEETING YOU AT
PAUL'S WALDEN, and the more so, as the post
brought ME no reason for that disappointment. I
had MANY THINGS TO SAY TO YOU, exclusive of a
wish to renew those social hours, from which I have
hitherto felt so much gratification. I can account
for your profession though not for your pen. However this instant I have had a blow, which in the
annals of friendship must have struck deep, could
I have formed such an opinion of you, as to allow
it even for a moment, the most distant foundation.
An idea of that kind was impossible, because, by
your letters respecting my late request, my knowledge of your kindness upon all occasions, and that
general character which you bear, all join to con-
tradict it. Lady Strathmore who is now by me,
and who has been snatched from her villainous
domestics by a COUP-DE-GRACE, to which I REGRET
I HAVE BEEN SO LITTLE INSTRUMENTAL, informs
me, " that I have often been deceived in my friendship, and that she would assure me I never was
more so than in the present instance ; and, as a

I 4

point in question, she knew that the application I
had made to you to take a house in London, produced the following expression : ' Damn me, if I
will take a house for Bowes, lest I should have it
to pay for.' " I am so well convinced, my dear
Sir, that this story was fabricated to impose upon
Lady Strathmore (for some purpose) that I repeat
my wishes, that you would soon procure me a
house of £300 per annum ; and that you will assure
yourself, how much

I am,

Your sincere friend and humble servant,

A. R. BOWES.

I perfectly recollect having made use of the very
expression which the Countess told to Bowes : and
the Countess was told of what I said by my friend
of Palace-yard, to whom I had imparted it.   He
had been reconciled to the Countess after she eloped
from Bowes, and after the relatives and friends of
the late Lord had taken up her cause.   As I have
explained it, this curious fact affords matter for con-
templation.   It must be clear that there had been
a familiar conversation between them : and what is
more curious, is, that this letter Bowes sent to me,
is dated on the 11th, the day after his seizing the
Countess, although the post mark on it was the
21st, so that even then, THERE WAS A FAMILIAR
CONVERSATION BETWEEN THEM.

We, ignorant of ourselves, beg often our own
harm, which the wise powers deny us for our good

Shakespeare so says: did not Bowes think at least what might befal him!!

I shall now proceed with a detail of what farther came within my own PERSONAL KNOWLEDGE.

On Thursday, November the 23d, just before the sitting of the Court of King's Bench, the Countess of Strathmore was brought into Westminster Hall, and immediately on the arrival of the Judges, Mr. Law, her counsel, moved, that she might be permitted to exhibit articles of the peace against Mr. Bowes and several others; which being granted, he then moved for an attachment against Bowes and several of his accomplices, which was likewise granted. And on the 27th, Bowes was also arrived at BARNET in his way to London, and in custody. from whence he wrote the following

LETTER.

From A. R. Bowes, Esq. to Jesse Foot, Esq.

BARNET, *Tuesday Morning*, 5 *o'clock.*

MY DEAR SIR,

I beg to see you immediately, as I am in real necessity for your professional abilities, and I am so distressed in body, that nothing but a mind fully convinced of its own rectitude could support it. Before the cock crows thrice, my enemies shall be convinced that I paid more attention to my LATE movements, than their present eclat gives them an idea of---Nemo mortalium omnibus horis sapit.

I am ever yours,

A. R. BOWES.,

Before I had scarcely finished the perusal of this letter, Bowes drove to my house, but without getting out of the chaise, put up at Atkinson's hotel, in Dean-street. His beard was a week old, his head bound up with a bloody handkerchief, his boots dirty, his shirt and cravat stained with blood, and he looked as pale as ashes. I mulled him some wine; but his stomach rejected it. He wanted not to go down to Westminster Hall, the men who had him in custody wanted him to go; he solicited me to go down to prove his sickness. I told him I would, if he could get another to join me. We sent to Dr. Kennedy, late physician to the army, who with me, advised him by all means to go down, and at length he complied, and I accompanied him. He was twice sick in the coach, and as his wound was on his head, I began to think whether his skull might not have been fractured, but he had no other ominous and indicative symptoms of fracture but vomiting merely.

When he passed through the Hall, he was saluted with hisses; and after a very little time having passed, and the legality of the service being established, and his counsel having proposed that he should not be committed in his present state, as there was no accommodation in a prison for a man so ill, the Marshall said, in a loud tone, that he could ACCOMMODATE THE GENTLEMAN; the Court all laughed out aloud; and poor Bowes was clapped into the coach which was waiting for him, and hurried over to the King's Bench, and the Marshall was ready to open the state rooms for the accommodation of his prisoner.

The first three weeks, after his admission into this place, were taken up with those adjustments which are found necessary for all who seek for comfort in such abodes of accommodation. His wounds being examined, appeared to be healing; but they were deep and long, and would have been deeper, had not the skull put a limitation to the blows. I found out the cause of his sickness and vomiting. The same disposition for intrigue and deception haunted him here, as it always had, just as if these qualities formed a part of his habit, and as if, from the organism of his frame, he could not be otherwise. He got a dose of ipecacuanha at Barnet, and took it just before I came into him at the hotel, PRIVATELY. This was done in order that his appearance might excite commisseration, and to avoid, if possible, being committed to a prison.

Bowes soon appeared to be reconciled to his condition, hope had not as yet abandoned him to despair. His plate was brought in, and his vanity was still about him; even at this time, I had not missed it; that and his deceptions took even now entire possession of him. The Court of King's Bench had not done with him; he and his accomplices were tried; and he, as a set off, or rather as a pretence for mingling his own case of real depravity, with an imaginary one of the Countess's, prosecuted her for perjury.

On Friday, 27th May, 1787, Andrew Robinson Bowes, Edward Lucas, Francis Peacock, Mark Prevost, John Cummins, otherwise Charles Chapman, William Pigg, and three other persons, were tried in the Court of King's Bench, before Justice Buller, on an indictment, charging them with an assault committed on Friday the 10th day of November last, on the person of the Countess of Strathmore; after a trial of several hours, they were all found guilty. As soon as the trial was over, Bowes, by the advice of Mr. Erskine, withdrew the indictment he had preferred against the Countess for perjury. Bowes preferred a second indictment against the Countess, which was heard in July, but which failed also.

On the 26th of June, 1787, Andrew Robinson Bowes, Edward Lucas, Francis Peacock, Mark Prevost, and Henry Bourn, were, pursuant to order, brought up to receive judgment for a conspiracy, of which they were convicted in April last, against the Countess of Strathmore; the reading of the several affidavits took up almost four hours; after the counsel on both sides had concluded, Judge Ashurst pronounced the sentence of the Court as follows :---

Majesty; that he be imprisoned in his Majesty's
prison of the King's Bench for three years, and at
the expiration of the said term, he find security f(r
fourteen years, himself in £10,000 and two sureties
of £5,000 each.

That Edward Lucas (the constable) do pay a
fine of £50, and be imprisoned in his Majesty's
gaol of Newgate for the term of three years.

That Francis Peacock do pay a fine of £100,
and be imprisoned in the King's Bench prison for
two years.

That Mark Prevost be imprisoned in the goal of
Newgate for one year, no fine.

That Henry Bourn do pay a fine of £50, and be
imprisoned in the gaol of Newgate for six months.

Lucas, Peacock, and Prevost, were already under bail, by order of the Court of King's Bench,
themselves in £500, together with two sureties in
the sum of £250 each, for keeping the peace towards the Countess of Strathmore for fourteen
years.

Bowes, upon another application, had a remis-
sion of the fourteen years to two.

The conspirators being thus disposed of, Bowes
becoming habituated to the situation, and all those
incumbrances upon his mind being cleared away,
after his usual manner, in their turns, he discarded

every one of those conspirators as soon as he had done with them, and he left them to their fates. The poor French valet, Prevost, fractured his collarbone in Newgate, and underwent much distress afterwards, without money or character.

It may be difficult to be believed; but I do not think that any one of the conspirators knew what they risqued, when they were instrumental in this act of violence, except Lucas; I do not think that even the ruined Peacock did; but of him I shall have to speak hereafter.

Having thus cleared the proceedings of the conspiracy, than which no revolution can present bolder and deeper traits, I come now to describe the Life of Bowes, for the last twenty-two years, first of all in the state rooms, next in inferior state rooms, then within the walls of the Bench, and about the last twelve years, within the rules in St. George's Fields.

The two leading occupations of his time consisted of his law affairs, and his seductions; in relating the former, I am afraid I shall be bewildered, from want of technical knowledge; and in the latter, I shall contrive to be as much upon my guard, and as frugal as I can of all obscenity.

Bowes's family in the King's Bench, at first consisted of himself, Mr. and Mrs. Peacock and daughter, and Master Bowes, his son, by the Countess. Besides other requisite servants, he had brought up one of the name of MARY, who waited on the Countess during the time Bowes took her into the North ; and when she was taken from him, Bowes secured Mary. She was a good-hearted, hard working woman, and possessed more than a common share of the homely and useful qualities; her he seduced, and sent her away to lye-in, and then abandoned her, and the child also not long afterwards. This was the woman he dress-ed up to personate the Countess.

For the first twelvemonths of his imprisonment, there was scarcely a day that I was not over there, on account of some professional call or other; there-fore I had an opportunity of seeing all his move-ments during this period; the most restless, and perhaps the most crowded with concerns, and of the most importance to him, of any part of his life. Either he was to come again out of the prison after the expiration of three years, as a great man, or be finally fixed for ever after, as a crushed and misera-ble one.

The vast consumption of money, which those up-hill law proceedings demanded, he had not cal-culated upon: as I have said, he received his death's blow of hope of ever recovering any of the Bowes's property, in the Court of King's Bench, whilst the Countess was in the hands of Mr. Shuter and Mr. Seton: the attorney who succeeded them, followed up the advantage, of which they originally had been the pioneers.

Soon after Bowes was married to the Countess,

he discovered that she had contrived and signed a deed, which was dated just one week before the ceremony took place, whereby she made a settlement of the estates which had been willed to her by her father, so as to place the rents and produce of those estates at her own disposal, whether she should be single or married, reserving to herself a power to revoke and annul this deed.

It is very reasonable and natural to suppose, that any man in the character of a husband would get rid of such a settlement if he could; and it is generally believed, indeed it has been sworn that Bowes was not very gentle in the mode which he adopted in accomplishing his purpose. Be that as it may, the Countess of Strathmore, by an instrument under her hand and seal, bearing date the 1st of May, 1777, rather less than four months after the marriage, revoked the obnoxious settlement.

The Countess at the time of the marriage was considerably in debt, and willing to raise a fund to discharge those debts, and not as has untruly been stated, to apply the money to Bowes's use. The Countess and Bowes joined in a deed, granting annuities to the yearly amount of £3,000 for the Countess's life. By this measure was raised a sum of £24,000. In order to secure the payment of these annuities, certain parts of the estates in which the Countess had a life interest, were vested in trustees, in trust to receive the rents, and out of the rents to pay the annuities, and to pay the overplus and residue, if any, to Bowes and the Countess. This is the substance of the deed.

In the year 1785 the Countess instituted a suit in the Court of Chancery against Bowes, charging him with various acts of cruelty and outrage, and setting forth that the instrument of revocation was extorted from her by violence and compulsion; and praying the Court to restrain Bowes from receiving the rents of her estates. After various litigations the cause came to a hearing, and the Court directed what is technically called an issue, to be tried in a court of law by a jury, to ascertain whether the deed of revocation was obtained in the manner represented by the Countess.

It was to this trial in the Court of Common Pleas, before Lord Rosslyn, which was immediately to come on, that all Bowes's hopes and fears were directed. The consequence of the verdict was, that the instrument of revocation was deemed a nullity, and upon the final hearing of the suit in Chancery, first before Judge Buller, sitting for the Lord Chancellor Thurlow, and afterwards before Lord Thurlow himself, the settlement, called the antenuptial deed was established; and it was referred to a master in Chancery to take an account of rents received by Bowes since the commencement of the suit, upon which account a large sum was reported due by the master, and the master appointed a person to be the receiver of the rents and profits of the estates of the Countess.

K

Thus I have endeavoured to state the case of the trial at issue before Lord Rosslyn, and it was at this trial that the circumstances of the deed were introduced, and that the whole series of acts of cruelty, violence, and compulsion, were proved.

As soon as the event of this trial found its way to Bowes, for the first time, perhaps, in his whole life, he began to sink into the most complete state of despondency. Every faculty seemed to have deserted him, but his deception. He pretended lameness, and took to his bed, saw scarcely any body, and kept himself in a constant state of intoxication. I was obliged to remonstrate with him upon his cowardice, and told him that I suspected he meant by drinking, to put a period to himself; but that it was a very base way, and that it would take a long time before he would succeed, if that were his object, by the quantity he now took; and that there were other ways, if he wanted to give his enemies a triumph, and to gratify them, by his funeral knell, WITH A ROUT FOR THE COUNTESS, AND WITH A CAROUSAL FOR HIS LAW OPPONENTS, WITH A BONFIRE FOR THE CONFESSIONS, AND A CARNIVAL AT GIBSIDE.

Another deadly blow followed also. The sentence of separation and divorce now issued from Doctors Commons, and he was stunned with the thunder, of excommunication. He was charged with the sums he had unjustly received from these estates, and they were entered on the Marshall's

books.   Thus mauled, stripped, disgraced, and
blasted, the prison bolts flew open; all of a sudden
he bad adieu to the outer state rooms, and entered
within the walls, in a pickle not unmerited, and in
a state which to some, death would have been com-
paratively an ELYSIUM.

The Countess animated by her liberation from
the tyrannical power of Bowes, in the effusion of
her blissful meditation of freedom, composed and
sent the following triumphant composition upon
Bowes's privation of power over her, written in the
form of an epitaph, of which the following is the
TRUE COPY, FROM HER OWN HAND.

An Epitaph wrote and sent by LADY STRATH-
MORE to A. R. BOWES in the KING'S BENCH
PRISON.

HERE RESTS,
Who never rested before,
The most ambitious of men :
For he sought not virtue, wisdom, or
Science, yet rose by deep hypocrisy,
By the folly of some,
And the vice of others,
To honours which Nature had forbid,
And riches he wanted taste to enjoy.
He saw no faults in himself,
Nor any worth in others.
He was the enemy of mankind;

Deceitful to his friends,
Ungrateful to his benefactors,
Cringing to his superiors,
And tyrannical to his dependents.
　　If interest obliged him to assist
Any fellow creature, he regretted the
Effect, and thought every day lost
In which he made none wretched.
　　His life was a continual series
Of injuries to society,
Disobedience to his Maker,
And he only lamented, in despair .
That he could offend them no longer.
　　He rose by mean arts
To unmerited honours,
Which expire before himself.
　　Passenger, examine thy heart,
If in aught thou resemblest him ;
And if thou dost——
Read, tremble, and reform !
So shall he, who living
Was the pest of society,
When dead, be, against his will,
Once useful to mankind.

Every body can tell, that within the walls of the
King's Bench Prison the vices would' be more
circumscribed, but the heart would not be mended.
By this time Peacock and Bowes were at drawn
daggers. Peacock's instrumentality was over.
Richard wanted Buckingham no longer. The un-

fortunate and credulous Peacock had been a most respectable coal merchant at Newcastle. He became acquainted with Bowes at his election. He was a tall athletic man, proper qualities for elections, easy of persuasion, and vain of Bowes's confidence. He projected nothing, but obeyed him in every thing. Besides his punishment by imprisonment and fine, having joined Bowes in acceptances, he was left in the lurch by Bowes, and remained in the prison, and within the rules of it, for years afterwards.

The friend to whom Bowes addressed all his letters, who rescued Lady Maria from his bitter gripe, who preserved the jewels for the family's splendor, who in obedience to the mandate of the Lord Chancellor, made two journies to France at his own cost, to bring back Lady Anna Maria; who waited days at LISLE, on his first journey unsuccessfully, by Bowes pretending to be sick; who drew upon himself the Lord Chancellor's censure on not being able to do what his Lordship's power and authority could not; had from these causes at this time withdrawn himself, and abandoned Bowes to his merited fate. This friend, who had thus been put to a great expence in his two journies, who had brought back Lady Anna Maria, and restored her to the bosom of her friends, who had served the family, by preserving the jewels, who had obeyed the Chancellor, and would, if possible, have kept Bowes within the pale of honesty, was suspected and censured on all sides : and thus reputation may be likened to the positive and nega-

tive powers of electricity; where the best disposed
man may lose his character by too near an approx-
imation to a bad one.

Bowes now, like a tree struck by lightning, had
still a few green branches left. He had the best
room within the walls of the prison, and as birds
do, when they are reconciled to the cage, he began
to plume himself up, to peck, and meditate upon
the possible smiles the place could afford him.   He
took an analysis of the inhabitants, and particularly
all those he could make useful to his purpose, he
tempted by his dinners.   I saw one gentleman at
Bowes's table, whom I have known ever since, for
whom I still entertain the highest regard, and who
could have written this life much better than I am
able.

On the 13th July, 1787, Bowes desired me to
visit a young girl, the daughter of a prisoner, at the
lodgings of her mother in Lant Street. I found her
a girl of perfect symmetry, fair, lively, and innocent.
She was feeding a pidgeon with split peas out of
her mouth. She had a little fever from summer
heat and bad air. Her father in the prison had
been a man of considerable landed property, he
had kept a pack of hounds entirely at his own
expence, in opposition to a neighbour, and a rival,
who kept a pack at that time also. They had
literally hunted each other down. But this gentleman, at this time, had not parted with his estate.

Bowes having seen this girl pass through the

prison to her father's apartments, whose charms of
attraction, when they caught his eye, served but
insidiously to betray her to him, who like a roaring
lion, sought night and day whom he could devour,
addressed her going and coming, made her pre-
sents, flattered, and obtained her.   The father died
shortly afterwards, made a will, and left Bowes his
executor, but it is not known whether he ever acted
upon it.

This young lady, whom I shall call Miss Polly
S---, has had five children by him, which proved to
be ties of such strong affection as to soften all the
hardships and severities she has so long endured ;
for she has been literally a prisoner in his house
from the year 1787 to the day of his death.   He
hired a room for her in the same staircase, where
she was excluded from the sight of every body, not
being seen even at his dinners, nor morning, noon,
nor night.   She " went in a maid, but out a maid .
never departed more," not even to revisit the
glimpses of the moon.

Upon the sickness of her children, I happened to
see her a few times, but it was impossible to say
one word more to her than what belonged to the
case, as Bowes was always present, hurried the
visit as much as possible, locked the door, and took
the key in his pocket.   She was blessed with a
native chearful disposition, and had found a chan-
nel for her affections in her children.   She had ever
been herself a child of misfortune ; all which parti-

culars marked, adapted and qualified her for being
a true and rare representative OF A FEMALE OF FOR-
TITUDE.

Bowes had an inquisitive turn for knowing every
person of any importance within the walls; but all
those he was desirous of insinuating himself into
their favour, did not readily accept his solicitations.
Some who were there from misfortunes, and not
from crimes, did not choose to associate with him.
For although the law has made no separate distinction of apartments between the criminal and the
unhappy debtor, yet the mind of the debtor may be
above the connection of the criminal. Upon these
grounds, there were, I am persuaded, some who
knowing his character, were shy of his society.
There happened to be two or three considerable
people of this description, who soon after his arrival, found themselves frequently assailed and privately lampooned and vilified without being ever
able to trace those gross attacks to their origin.

I have been told the following anecdote of Bowes.
The father of Miss Polly S------ had found a man
in the prison, who attributed his confinement in a
great measure to a debt that was due from him.
Whenever they met, they were seen to wrangle and
exchange accusations. Bowes hearing this repeatedly pass, one morning called on Mr. S------, and
proposed to him to feign himself dead, on purpose
to see what the man would say upon it. The bed
cloaths were taken off, Mr. S------ was laid out, his
chin tied up, and the sheet placed over him. Bowes

then went in search of the man; upon finding him,
he communicated what had befallen his enemy,
Mr. S——; the man did not seem disposed to believe him, when Bowes insisted that he should come
and convince himself. Accordingly this violent,
man, whose debt would now be certainly lost, hastened to see, and thinking it too true, poured over
the body vollies of abuse, and continued to do so
for an aggravating time, till at length Mr. S——
could submit to the farce no longer, but threw off
the sheet, and rose up in the bed, when the affrighted man made a sudden escape.

A near relation of Bowes paid him a visit in the
King's Bench, just at a time when a very fine and
conspicuous lady was liberated from the same place.
It was to be so contrived, that she visited Bowes
in her own handsome equipage, when this relation
was with him. Bowes gave the relation to understand, that she was a rich widow, possessing in her
own right not less than £40,000. In a day or two
after, Bowes as a favour done to his relation, agreed
that he, with a friend of Bowes's, should call upon
this lady, and carry with them their introduction
from himself to her. They found her in a very elegant house in Abington Street, and richly furnished, She apologized for the want of servants,
as she said, they were almost all in the country, it
being summer time, The friend who accompanied
Bowes's relation, was perfectly satisfied that neither
the house, furniture, equipage, nor servants belonged
to this lady, and from compassion hinted to the relation, that it was better for him to desist in this pur-

suit, but that he was not to impart this opinion he gave, to Bowes. The relation very fortunately was wise enough to take advice, and in consequence of this intimation, the pursuit was dropped. Although this story might appear mysterious, yet a little thought will shew what was meant by Bowes. His relation was a man of property, and if Bowes could have made up a match between them, he would have had a bond from the lady before marriage, and brought it against his relation after marriage.

An amorous gentleman's chamber in the King's Bench, happened to be facing the window of the apartments where Miss Polly S---------- resided. Bowes thinking that he might pay her too assiduous an attention from one window to the other, for he never could by any other means have ever done more, dressed himself up in a female habit, and flirted with this gentleman at the window. This he repeated for many successive mornings, and had satisfactorily engaged the gentleman's attention. When he had worked up his plot, and brought his deception to the proper pitch, Bowes threw open the window, shook off the female dress, and displayed his own proper person, laughing, insulting, and jeering by breaths, as he could do in a manner to confound those whom he had caught in his toil. The poor amorous man was so disconcerted, that he was not visible for a long time after.

Bowes had a practice which he applied whenever he could, if he wanted to make any part of his com pany drunk, and as far as I have seen, he was generally successful. I have known very grave people over whom he has so succeeded. He would appear to be very candid, and to tell his guests they should help themselves to the spirits which were upon the table, whilst he officiously poured the water to fill up the glasses out of the tea kettle. All this appeared very fair, but he had instructed his servant to bring in the kettle, with half and half of water and spirits, so that the more his guests were desirous of being sober, the drunker they became.

Bowes experienced not a little gratification and exhilaration of spirits by an occurrence which afforded him some agreeable pastime, and exonerated his mind from dwelling for awhile upon his OWN miseries, by filling it up with the pleasures of ANOTHER'S.

He was addressed by letter, by the lady of the brother of the attorney, who conducted the cause of the Countess against him; of the brother whom Bowes had turned out of the carriage at Highgate at the time he violently seized the Countess's person. He published a phamplet in the lady's name, insinuating that she had lost the affection of her husband by the intrigue of the Countess. Bowes took the lady into his apartments, and succoured and encouraged her in her action, till he succeeded and brought the gentleman to a settlement with the lady. This flattered him, but procured for him no other advantage.

As no man is certain when he offers injuries to another, that even-handed justice may not return the poisoned chalice to his own lips, so it happened in a short time after to Bowes; some bills of indictment, by the prisoners, were found against him at the Croydon Assizes, which gave him a great deal of trouble, and incurred some expence; but by the address of his attorney, he was acquitted, and this threatening ignominy corrected his future demeanour.

Bowes, at this time, drew part of his subsistence from a share in a coal ship, and shipped his own coals for the London market, and sold them by his own agents. The unfortunate and injured Peacock had been induced by the opinion of his lawyer, to consider this, as dealing in coals, and to consider Bowes as a coal dealer, and as one liable to the laws of bankruptcy. Accordingly a commission of bankruptcy was taken out against Bowes in 1798, and his name appeared in the gazette. His commission was regularly opened at Guildhall; but on the sitting of the Lord Chancellor, Rosslyn, it was proved before his Lordship that Bowes's dealings extended no farther than his selling his own coals out of his own ship, the commission from that cause was set aside to poor Peacock's cost and disappointment.

Bowes having very lately mustered up a little more courage, began to meditate upon a renewal of his law proceedings, and in order that he might have more justice done to him, than he had in the conduct of his former suit, as he suspected, at least, he had engaged a new attorney, Mr. Palmer of Grays Inn, a gentleman of erudition in literature in general, of acute observation, good address, and high reputation.

Under this gentleman's auspices, he commenced a suit in the Court of Chancery, about the year 1797, claiming the surplus rents of the estates set apart to pay the annuities, to which the Countess put in no answer. Bowes then applied to the House of Lords, whose decision was in his favour. Elated by this, he recurred again to the Court of Chancery, under the expectation that he was certain of success, to the amount of, at least, £60,000; that he was so certain, he had now advertised for sale a part of the property.

Previous to this event, the Countess had departed this life on the 20th of April, 1800. The cause thus standing, revived, there could be no question raised whether Bowes were entitled or no to all that was settled upon, or limited to him and his wife, during their joint lives. But admitting that Bowes was entitled to the estate so settled and limited, yet by the death of the Countess, Bowes met with the opposition of the Earl of Strathmore and the other executors of the Countess, and therefore the same claim was revived by Bowes on the 12th of February, 1802 against her executors in the Court of Chancery. But eventually all these petitions by Bowes were dismissed, there having been made by Lord Rosslyn during his time of being Chancellor a LATENT ORDER.

THE LATENT ORDER was heard, and reheard; and the result of it was, that there was an issue some time after to try in one of the Courts below the validity of the instrument of revocation, which was made four months after the marriage of Bowes to the Countess, whether this instrument under which Bowes claimed, was not extorted from her by violence, and compulsion: of the event of all this, I shall speak hereafter.

It is my duty here to observe, that Mr. Scott, who formerly had been Bowes's counsel, and to whose name Bowes had so often referred in his letters to his friend from Paris, was the now Lord Eldon, the Lord Chancellor, before whom the revived litigation was to be heard, he having succeeded the Lord Rosslyn, and that Lord Eldon, from motives of the nicest delicacy, upon the hearings of the Lord Rosslyn's LATENT ORDER, called the master of the Rolls, Sir William Grant, to be present with him during the hearing of this cause.

I have now left the proceedings in this state without pursuing them any further as yet, to the event of the time yet to come. For if I went on with that now, which was not finally concluded till some time after, I should not only be guilty, being out of season, of an anachronism, but also of confounding the order of the narrative. Besides, as it so happened, the delay was all on Bowes's side. It

served to keep up his spirits and appearance; it
gave him credit with those from whom he wanted
it; and the assurance he really possessed, or artfully
feigned, of eventual success, did not fail to increase
his spirits not a little, but his pecuniary resources a
great deal.

Upon the death of the Countess, Bowes moved
out of the prison, and took a house in the London
Road, in St. George's Fields. Mr. Palmer under-
took, by a sort of tontine, to fill up the ·requisite
securities for Bowes's debt to the satisfaction of the
Marshal. Then here we see Bowes once more out
of prison, but not out of danger. He took all his
family with him, Miss S. the children, and all his
dogs and cats, of which he had more than a common share, and which he kept very poor.

The law suits were taking their course. He
began to embrace the liberty of reviving those
sentiments of seduction, which had been from
want of convenience laid by, and become dormant
during his closer confinement. He took another
house also on the Borough Road in St. George's
Fields, to which there was attached a pretty garden, and next to a billiard room. This he gave
out was to supply his family; at any rate he took
care that it should furnish him with his means of
supplying a family. Whatever might have been
the quantity or quality of inhabitants, whether
tenants in common or proper, I am not exactly able
to enumerate; but the history of one of his tenants
I am perfectly well acquainted with.

A very neat and modest young woman, a semp-
stress, visited her sister in the King's Bench, who
was associated to a gentleman there, a clergyman.
Bowes used to, every now and then, cast a longing
and a lingering look towards the interior of these
walls, and thus fell in with this fair visitor. He
succeeded in his addresses, and placed her in this
convenient house in the Borough Road. There
she remained during her pregnancy, and she was
always associated with the eldest or the other of
his own daughters, by Miss S. They took their
station there by turns. Bowes, the only time he
had ever liberated her, had now given Miss S. permission to go to see her mother, and attempted to
bring this girl into his house, in her absence, but on
her arrival, his own daughters resisted it: they left
him, and fled to their mother. Bowes fearful that
this transaction would become public, and that the
case of Miss S------'s usage would be a matter of
advantage to his law opponents, and possibly, that
she might have their support in preferring her
grievances, gave way, the only time he was ever
known to do so. Mrs. S------ with her daughters,
returned, and the girl was dismissed from this
house to go back to the other, where she was
brought to bed.

Bowes had promised to settle upon her two
hundred pounds per annum, but now as she was
brought to bed of a live child, he offered her fifty
pounds more if she would swear the child to a
gentleman in the Bench, confined for debt. She
did swear the child to that gentleman, and he was

not liberated till he paid the fine to the parish so imposed; after this Bowes discarded and abandoned the unfortunate and corrupted girl.

Just after the success in the House of Lords, and when the cause was revived in the Court of Chancery by this spirited and friendly solicitor, Bowes had an accession to his property in Ireland, a freehold of the value of three hundred pounds per annum. From this, and from the remnant of plate, of which there was yet a huge mass, and from his half pay, he might have drawn a decent subsistence. His BENWELL estate was in the hands of receivers, for the mortgagee, therefore he could take nothing from that, though if it were sold it would fetch three times the sum for which it was mortgaged.

I have stated this to shew the disposition and the art of Bowes. He would make a grand display of all this property, produce the reports of surveyors who had valued it, and profess to come to a speedy resolution to sell. And, I ought to observe, that in the display of this property there was no falsehood. The falsehood consisted in the professed use he made of this display. He pretended to sell, but never intended it. He pleaded most pressingly his immediate wants, his own tattered appearance, and the state of his children, which he so contrived, that they may be seen without shoes or stockings; and also his want of means of prosecuting his law suit, adding, that if he had money now it could be repaid on the sale of his property. He would even fix a time that the sale should take place. In this practice, perhaps, there never was a more perfect adept; as I do not know an instance in which he did not succeed to a certain degree. This was the game he played for the last ten years of his life, and always more or less coming off a winner.

At the end of twelve years service, his solicitor, Mr. Palmer, was obliged to give him up, and this cancelled every obligation Bowes owed him; for he was unremittingly, every time I saw him, pouring forth abuse on Mr. P. for thus forsaking him, though he repeatedly sent for him to return to him, but in vain.

I have stated what Bowes practised to get money from his attorneys; and now I will shew how he used to get over the fulfilment of his promise to reimburse all those credulous attorneys, who were in advance for him. He invariably practised the trick of being ill, of having lost his faculties, his memory, and his hearing. He would cause the attorneys to understand by messages, that if they came to transact business with him, it may endanger his life.

In one of these situations, he sent for me; on my arrival he affected not to know me; I was to speak very softly; the barber was sent for; he was to describe to me the fit he had had; whilst the barber was describing the fit, he fell into one before us both. This farce being over, he began to mend, and to expose his intention, which was to get me to

inform his attorney of the extreme dangerous state
of his health

In a very short time after this part of the farce
had been played, and just as I was preparing to go,
a neighbour's cock came into his yard, and was
fighting with one of his own. His eldest son was
ordered to drive out the cock; in doing this, there
was a great uproar among the fowls, and that uproar
lasted for some time. The strange cock flew twice
against Bowes's window; and from his affectation
of low speaking, we could not hear each other for
the noise. When Bowes of a sudden started up as
strong as Hercules, threw up the sash, and bawled
out to his son just as vociferously as he ever could
have done at any time of his life. Without uttering
a single syllable by way of comment, I left him to
his own reconciliation.

But this is only one way in which he practised these
deceptions; others equally ingenious will succeed
in their turn. The next attorney he had was of a
short duration; but long enough to make a journey
to take a survey of his estates, and to become responsible for his house rent.

During the time of the succeeding attorney's attendance, (the third) there were such a series of impositions practised, as perhaps were never known,
or heard of: but the detail of them, I shall defer for
the present, to give room for another instance, which
comes in rotation as part of the supplies upon
which Bowes was now subsisting; as he embraced

every means he possibly could to obtain the property of others without lessening his own. This was his system.

I am told that the half pay of an officer is so settled, that no deed he can execute for the sale of it, can invalidate his recovering it, whenever on its becoming due he goes and claims it. Bowes knew this, and therefore he could sell this part of his property, as he thought, without lessening his own. He continued receiving his half pay, notwithstanding, just the same after the sale of it, as he did before. But eventually he found himself mistaken. The creditor's courage was rouzed. He brought his action, gained his cause, obtained an execution, and recovered all his money. To raise this sum, Bowes, who had never calculated upon such an event, and who did not dream of what this creditor could have done to him, as finally he could have fixed him in Newgate, was driven to his last shift. But he must now pay this creditor, who had been an overmatch for him. He was obliged to part with the remainder of the family plate, with rings, gold snuff boxes, watches, and all the rich dresses, made up for him, when he was at PARIS, and which his vanity had kept till now, enough to stock all the theatres, for THE SIR GEORGE AIRIES, THE LOVEMORES, THE LORD FOPPINGTONS, and THE RANGERS, in the most extensive theatrical district throughout this country.

Though this transaction was not finally concluded till Bowes had engaged another attorney,

(his fourth) yet, as it commenced with his third attorney, it was better to state it here as a part of his
ways and means. The last act of this kind attorney
was to draw up Bowes's WILL, he being pleased to
be thought very ill indeed at that time. And I am
now to exhibit a specimen of Bowes's natural disposition for feigning sickness, and which he practised on his sister as a return for her affectionate
visit to him, in order to get, if he could, from her
husband a larger annuity, on account of the pretended precarious state of health. This I shall call
his ANNUITY SICKNESS.

One of Bowes's SISTERS came from IRELAND
with her daughter, to partake of the advantage of
the southern education for this most promising
young lady. His sister's object was to have
teachers for her in all the desirable branches of
modern education here, for a short time, and also to
entertain a governess to accompany them from
hence to Ireland as one of the family. Bowes's
sister appeared to me to be sincere, virtuous, intelligent, and strictly consonant and guided by the
best discipline of the best regulated families, among
the best class of modern society. I had the pleasure of seeing her every day for three months, and,
as these visits were made painful to me from
Bowes's conduct, there could not possibly be any opportunity for me to arrive at a knowledge of her more
accomplished virtues than from what I saw in my
daily visits to Bowes. Instead of taking up her residence in a more select situation, she, from wishing to
be near her SUFFERING BROTHER, took a lodging

opposite to him.   Bowes never said a word more
to me, than that she was his sister.   Every quality
about her was to be made out from my own observation.

At this time Bowes WAS PLEASED TO BE VERY ILL
INDEED.   He was dropsical, he had shortness of
breath, loss of appetite; he vomited blood, his
languor was excessive, his nerves were easily irritated; he could attend to no concerns, neither upon
law matters, nor in his domestic œconomy.   Miss
S------ was of so depraved a nature, that she stained
his fair fame, by being an involuntary resident in
his family; the violence of her nature was such that
his mind was under her most compleat dominion.
A quarrel was excited, upon the entrance of his sister, as a pretext for Miss S------'s cruelty and authority over him.   A book was lost of the utmost
value, (the confessions) Miss S------, had stolen it;
and secreted it.   Whatever more may be imagined
to amplify this report of Bowes's complaint against
Miss S------, may be put into the catalogue,   The
children were all neglected, and their miserable ap-
pearances and deficiencies of education were all at
the door of the JEZABEL MISS S------.   His infirmities, and his miserable domestic situation, ren-
dered him incapable of performing any of the most
ordinary transactions of life.   If any thing was to
be PAID, or BOUGHT, or done of any kind, the RE-
FERENCE was made over the way to his SISTER,
If any proposition was made for his health, either
by prescription or direction, his present capacity
was not in a state to attend to it; the sister must be

instructed upon it. Miss S------ was too vicious, unfeeling, and abandoned for having any share in any part of this his most dangerous state of bodily health.

Every day I was desired to visit him and report the progress of his disorder to his SISTER. His body was measured to see if the dropsical tendency increased or diminished; the sister was to be informed of this, and was to see to the administration of the medicines. I was, always to attend him at the most valuable hour of the day, at one o'clock, and for two days following he vomited up BLOOD. After his going into another room, and after a cough of unaffected violence coming on, then I was called in to examine the BLOOD in the room, REAL BLOOD; and this was also to be reported to the sister, with a particular request to be tender and not to alarm her!

A man PLEASED to be so ill, in such a state, without any other strong inducement, must make a WILL. The third attorney was sent for, and hasty instructions were given him for the will, but not without apprehension that the subject may bring on agitation, and prematurely, from such a shock, endanger his life. The property of the countess, which was in litigation, BEING CERTAIN IN THE END, was included in the will, as well as all his other property. The children were all provided for. Miss S------'s name was not mentioned. Several legacies were bequeathed, and the rest of the property centered, in fair proportions, with his favoured relations, of which his sister was considered as a material and a chosen one. Even her daughter was mentioned in it with peculiar marks of affection. Such was this will, which Bowes LIVED to execute.

In the interim there was a negociation going forward relative to this FREEHOLD of his in Ireland. He wanted very much to dispose of it in his life time. He now wanted money or otherwise, as he did not wish it to go out of the family considering himself as a dying man, he would directly and most willingly make it over to his sister; but he even now wished that it should be called her own, and therefore, with a certain sum of money paid down, and with about a thousand a year during his SHORT STAY IN THIS WORLD, paid quarterly to him and very well secured in London, he would, without loss of time, surrender the estate in form to his sisters husband for his sister's use.

As it was a doubt whether the proposition could reach Ireland before the news that carried his death, it was, without delay, dispatched ; and as the answer to it bore naturally an urgency in proportion to the nature of the case, an answer was very soon returned, something to this effect: " that the husband thought it was indecent, and not becoming a relation, to take advantage in any bargain of a DYING man, not even in the shape and under the pretence of affection, and, therefore, he declined it altogether, hoping that his dear brother-in-law might long live to enjoy that, and all his other estates."

Bowes, a short time after, WAS PLEASED to begin to mend very fast, and his sister took leave of his neighbourhood, and lodged afterwards in Fludyer street. I had almost forgotten to explain one incident of this AFFECTING case, which is, that I was deceived in supposing that the blood, which I saw in the bason, and which, by his cough, Bowes was said to bring up from his lungs, was actually so discharged: Bowes had not then communicated to me, nor ever since, that he had procured FRESH CALVE'S BLOOD, and, by stealth, had gargled with it, and spat it into the bason. I ought also to remark that this WILL, which I saw then, has never since been heard of. In a subsequent one, and which has been acted upon, HE HAS NOT LEFT ONE SINGLE SHILLING TO HIS OWN RELATIONS.

The disappointment Bowes felt, from the answer of his sister's husband, gave a turn to his temper: after she was gone he appeared saucy and more vulgar in his manner than I had been used to; he gave broad hints that I stopped this design of his, but I had not, otherwise than by assuring his sister that I saw nothing about him which was so bad as he described. I never, in any other manner than through the sister, apprized her husband of the real state of Bowes's health, which never was BETTER THAN NOW. And it was a piece of information beyond his power of detection, which proved to my perfect satisfaction that he procured CALVE'S BLOOD. Indeed that is an old and stale trick. The same has been before detected amongst beggars, who practise it to excite compassion; and it is, I believe, to be found in CLARISSA HARLOW

This WILL had many intended operations. The children were now all christened in a lump. His sister insisted upon it that they should, finding that hitherto the ceremony had not been performed. Miss S., who never could have gone to a church by any possibility, nor out of her chamber, was here, also abused for her infidelity. The clergyman was put into this will. There were more than twenty friends, REAL FRIENDS, put into this will.

And here I shall remark a few curious facts. Bowes many times shewed me letters from a daughter of his, married to a gentleman resident in the country, which were well written, were full of affection, and always began and ended with, DEAR FATHER! There is also a daughter of his in Scotland, boarding with a clergyman, to whom arrears are due upon some years. The clergyman wrote several letters, but received no answer to them.

I have often seen Bowes carry about letters in his pocket, especially those he received from his counsel. And he has been known to shew them ten times over to the same person, at different times and at long intervals. He would thus use them, till their own weight would separate the folds into pieces, and till the paper was as dirty as a beggar's parish pass.

The WILL was sent over to his sister's lodgings, and there it remained to be referred to by all persons, whose good offices had contributed, for years or minutes, no matter which, to the generous purposes of gratifying and consoling long ago, or in his last moments, this DYING AND PENITENT CHRISTIAN.

The lease of the third attorney was now nearly expired. He was but a young man, and consequently, in the common phrase, soon done up. To him succeeded a fourth attorney, to whose firm was annexed a strong list of partnership. He took a cautious, no doubt, survey of Bowes's property; and if he did not, he might, have gone to see his possessions. But if he chose to dispense with this, Bowes was always warranted, I will say that for him, to assert, that he was a solvent man. This attorney assisted to Bowes's removal from the house in the London Road to one in the Lambeth Road, No. 12. It was in the month of January, 1804, that I first began to attend him during his ANNUITY SICKNESS, and which was brought on by his sister's visit to him, from the pure motive, as he said, of distinguishing her, and putting her into possession, of this family estate.

The beginning of the new attorney was a getting into troubled water, in the year 1805. The suit of the tradesman who purchased the half-pay was finally closed, so that Bowes had without any other concern almost a clear house. I do not now recollect that I was ever called to any sickness which it was Bowes's pleasure he should have, for a length of time; and this shews much better than I could otherwise prove it, that Bowes had been all along well supplied by his fourth attorney. If he, or some one as good, had not been answerable for the rent, how could Bowes have managed a landlord in St. George's Fields, and ever got honestly into another man's house?

The fourth attorney had an arduous task. THE CONSTANT CHANGE OF ATTORNIES DISHEARTENS THE BEST OF CAUSES. The rehearing of the LATENT ORDER left by Lord Chancellor Rosslyn, in the Court of Chancery, was conducted by him, and an issue was directed, by the Court, to be tried in a court of law before a jury, to ascertain whether the DEED of REVOCATION was obtained in the manner represented by the Countess of Strathmore. So that in fact, Bowes had not advanced one inch in his law proceedings, from their first commencement; as the very same cause had been tried in the Court of Common Pleas, before Lord Rosslyn, twenty years ago, which was now to be tried before Sir James Mansfield, in June 1807.

I being subpœned upon the trial, am able the better to give some report of it.

When the Court was prepared, Bowes's counsel stated that he wished to have the trial put off, as the Reverend Doctor Scott who resided upon his living in the North, and who witnessed the deed of revocation, was too ill to obey the subpœna. This being over-ruled, the case of the duel, of the marriage, and of the cruelties practised by Bowes on the Countess,. was as ably displayed, and in as eloquent a speech, so far as eloquence consists in the animation of facts, and in putting them with strength before a jury, as I have ever been accustomed to hear, by the leading counsel for the Earl of Strathmore. The first witness called was upon the subject of the DUEL; when the very same witness who formerly swore to the insignificance of the wounds, to there being scarcely any blood on the shirt, or perforation of it, swore the very same now. After him followed a long string of evidences by witnesses of various natures, by the living, who again proved ; and by the evidences of the dead, whose former testimonies were read in court, proved, and accepted: the case being thus made out, on the part of the Earl of Strathmore, Lord Eldon, who had been subpœned, and had been some time in Court, spoke as far as he had seen, handsomely to Bowes's character, and his Lordship withdrew.

His Lordship whilst his counsel had been instructed through Bowes only, he had only the opportunity, from the authority of his briefs, of seeing the superficies of his character, but was not furnished with any direction to speak upon a cubic knowledge of his heart; that was the concern of the Counsel against Bowes; and, to say the truth,

I never was more mentally gratified in all my life, than I was by observing the intellectual manner in which the sergeant for the Earl of Strathmore, exposed, and demonstrated this cause.

Bowes's Counsel made a reply, but called no witnesses; and then Sir James Mansfield addressed the jury, reciting the evidence, in its order, and with that perspicuity which marks the talent of an English lawyer, by which he rises to so eminent a situation through personal merit. The jury, without hesitation, pronounced the instrument of revocation to be a nullity, and a verdict was found in favour of the Earl of Strathmore. Here Bowes's contentions were finally resisted, if not positively concluded.

Bowes's antagonist in the duel was in the Court, he had been subpœned: he addressed the Court to be heard in answer to what the first witness had sworn, but ineffectually. Nor was I called to that part of the trial, or any other. Nor did I know if I had wanted to speak to him, nor should I now know the person of the attorney who conducted this cause. But it is fit to be remarked that neither the gentleman who fought the duel, nor myself, could have contradicted any part of the evidence, but merely that of the first witness.

I should now naturally proceed to make my remark upon the evidence of the first witness, had I not, when I was upon the subject of the duel, given all the explanation which may be deemed to be necessary.

From the time of this trial to the month of October, in the same year, I had not seen or heard from Bowes. He sent for me then in a desperate hurry, at eleven o'clock at night. Two of his children had putrid sore throats, and a third was in a disposition for a similar attack. Eventually they all recovered. He was obliged to admit me into the presence of Miss Polly S-----, but not one moment longer than he possibly could. And every time I called afterwards he took care I should hear none of her complaints, as he brought down the children to me.

It was midnight before I left his house. But he wanted to keep me longer, and to shew me his wine cellar, which I declined; the next, and next time I came, he pressed the same desire; again and again he pressed it. 'I could not account for why he thus pressed me to see the wine cellar of his dirty house; and as I usually called late at night, it struck me that possibly he meant to lock me up in it. To get rid of his teazing solicitations, I summoned courage to see this wine cellar, but I took care to keep behind him, and was upon my guard. I said jocularly to him, what in the fable, the crab said to his mother I PRÆ SEQUAR. He unlocked the door, and I very warily approached, just near enough to see his cellar full of wine. Oh! oh! said I to him, you have got a new and fifth attorney; a cellar full of wine; and a house without an execution in it!!! I have, said he, and then began, as it was his custom, to abuse the former attorney. I found that Bowes had his doubts whether when he sent for me I should come over to him or not; therefore, what with the wine and my visit, there was an assumed flow of merriment and wit in this convivial moment, but what was it, but the retrospection of the mind to the flavour of a mushroom nourished from a rotten dung hill!

In the next month, upon the opening of the Courts of Law, Bowes gave some action to his fifth attorney. He made an attempt to obtain a new trial, but all to no purpose. He, upon this occasion, wished me to call on the morning of this application, on his attorney, and meet him at his chambers. So that I went as much for my own interest as for his, especially as I was to meet him there, and of this he was very well aware. I did his business, but he took care not to do mine, as instead of coming into the chambers, he walked about the Square, and when he came to Westminster Hall he kept aloof, till I lost him.

All prospect of the Courts of Law affording Bowes any redress, was now become distant, and hardly discernible. Bowes then, being quite at leisure, for entertaining all the baser passions, improved upon them, as his health declined. Besides, he was circumscribed in his visits, and dared not go into the Bench.

I shall make a distinction at this time betwixt his general views as to his matters of property, and his amusements, and habits of life.

Bowes was decided that the estate of BENWELL HALL should not be sold during his life time, nor his estate in Ireland. To put off the evil day of parting with BENWELL, was what he always had most at heart. A prejudice of this sort,' for the preservation of a family estate, is sometimes so nearly allied to an affection for ancestry, that it approaches, if not assimilates itself, almost to a sense of virtue. But this was no family estate of his, and with him it can only be deemed an act of dishonesty, to keep his creditors out of their money, to make them as much as possible dependant on his will, and to defraud in the end as many of them as he could. When he engaged a fresh attorney, it was not only to carry on his suits, but to supply him with money; and it was in this manner he was using his fifth attorney.

As to his amusements, and his habits of life, they became baser as he grew older, and they were the more demonstrable, as he not only drank out his wine, selfishly, but also took to spirituous liquor. He kept no servant, and would buy neither brushes or brooms; the two daughters went down upon their knees and gathered up the dust with their hands; I have seen them describe this very humourously, laughing most heartily at this scene of necessity. He scarcely ever saw or spoke to Miss S---- for nearly the last eight years, and allowed her but one meal a day. She did get a little supply from her mother and the farmers, who had been her father's tenants. She had the strongest of all possi-

ble causes to remain with him; the children were
dear to her, and she to her children.

> "Déar as the light, that visits these sad eyes,
> Dear as the vital blood that warms this heart."

She was not disposed to be fretful, nervous, or
melancholy; she possessed a constancy and steadi-
ness of mind; she went through this pilgrimage of
distress, holding an even course; she had been
rocked in the cradle of adversity, and no ordinary
calamity could put her out of her way.

Bowes amused himself in instructing a copyist
to write letters to and from himself. To one creditor it was written that he had shot himself, and
that the person who wrote it, saw him weltering in
his blood. Another letter he carried about him, as
if it came from the Earl of Strathmore, offering him
terms of accommodation.

Bowes kept this man employed in this sort of business; so that the two instances which I have
given, should only be considered as specimens of
many more.

His passion for seduction had not now forsaken
him; the insolence of his mind would not submit to
the limitation to which his bodily infirmity restrain-
ed it. He had no longer a command over another's
affection, and the imposing art which gave life to
his seduction, no longer availed him. He could

dangle, but not possess; the lady he made up to was as knowing as himself; she surveyed him; but not admired him; to his character, she was no stranger, and paid him off in his own coin. His pockets were empty, and his march was feeble; his dress was shabby, and though no taylor's daughter, she knew that the nap of the best cloth would wear off; they were seen together too much in the public walks for the intrigue of lovers; they would in Term time come to Westminster Hall openly together; all this was hanging out lights of distress, by this fisher in troubled waters; he was literally generated into a slippered pantaloon. They soon quarrelled, and Bowes employed his copyist to go to work with his anonymous letters, and to carry on the contest on the lamp posts, watch boxes, and any other place where men adjourn. This lady was served quite right, for when she paraded up and down with him before his house, she knew that she was insulting a victim and a mother, locked up in a chamber up two pair of stairs.

Bowes's system for maintenance, had been so long supported by deception, that at length by the decay of his active bodily resources, he could not carry his mental ones into effect; he had all the inclination, without the ability, as a poisonous plant has in the WINTER, when the capillary attraction can no longer supply the nutrition that is necessary for the elaboration of its active and deleterious essence. He was sued for petty debts, and BENWELL HALL was about to be foreclosed. Those who were tired of his promises, broke out into violent discontent. He

could no longer play them. off with his usual success. He was besides entrammelled by fear, not
only present, but prospective; he dreaded the time
when the fifth attorney would stop his hand, and
that he may be obliged for want of house and furniture, to retire once more within the walls.

Under all this pressure, his suspicions of being
cheated, debarred him from receiving two hundred
pounds from Ireland whenever he pleased to sign
a receipt; but he would not sign it, and the agent
would not, but upon these terms, remit him the money.

His appetite began to fail, and his walk was confined to a tavern within four doors, where he used
to read a newspaper. As to his instruction, or
amusement from books, he had not one in his house
besides the CONFESSIONS; and I do not think that
he ever read a single book through, from the first
hour that he went into a prison, to the very last.

In the month of April, 1809, he made a WILL, and
he was by his FIFTH attorney, fairly and ingenuously, given to understand, that he would not advance him much more money.

The WILL he made in 1804, to amuse his sister,
and those to whom he had given such generous legacies, (as I have said) disappeared on the instant
of her departure. He opened a negociation with
another attorney; they had several interviews,
which proved to be ineffectual.

During the last summer, I had been several times informed that he was sinking, and that he had an inability to swallow, but upon a closer inquiry into this latter complaint from the person he sent, I was convinced that it was nothing but a new artifice branching out of an old system of imposition; yet from what I could collect of truth, though mixed with falsehood, I concluded that his end was approaching, as he then had real symptoms of dissolution, and of which he was not himself conscious; his legs swelled, and he had no appetite, and the wine being all drank out, he lived, by choice, upon rum and milk.

The WILL being signed in April, I don't believe the fifth attorney had any further intercourse with him to the time of his approaching death; and if he could have got any other to act, he would.

On the 10th of January, 1810, I was desired in great haste to visit Bowes, by his second son, and I could perceive from the natural manner of the youth, that it was no artificial alarm; therefore I most willingly obeyed the call. Miss S------ on my arrival opened the door to me, which she had never done before. Bowes expecting me, there was but little time allowed for me to hear what she had to say, before I must go into him, his bed being on the ground floor. She said that he had made a WILL since that he made which I knew of, that he had left something to all the children, but that her name was not in the will

Upon this, I was introduced to him, by her, and we were alone. It was apparent, that he had but a few days longer to live. I should not have known him, if I had seen him as a person of whom I had not been before apprised. I did not go round about with him, it was not a season for playing at push-pin, his case admitted of no trifling with time; I confessed to him my opinion of his situation, and asked of him to tell me if he had settled all his worldly affairs. Upon which Miss S------, said, he had made a will, and had within these two days given it to her to read, adding, that she would not find her name in it, but that it should be. She had sat up with him the last two nights; his eldest daughter used to officiate for him, but now, he would take nothing, nor accept of any office which was not done for him by Miss S------.

Seeing his dissolution so near, I did not urge him much then in behalf of Miss S------, as if he consented to give her any thing, I could not draw up the codicil. I asked loud enough for him to hear, who were his executors to the will? Miss S------ answered, the MARSHALL of the King's Bench Prison, and Mr. MEREDITH his attorney, of Lincoln's Inn.

Upon this, as there was no time to be lost, I made an excuse to go, promising to return again. I saw the Marshall of the King's Bench, and told him my errand, and intention of seeing him, to induce him to see Bowes, and prevail on him to leave something to Miss S------: The Marshall told me, that he did not know Bowes had nominated him as an executor, and therefore he did not see how he could, so situated, comply with my wishes ; but he hoped that I should be able to succeed. I then returned to Bowes, and took my leave of him, resolving to see Mr. MEREDITH, or his partner, Mr. ROBBINS, of Lincoln's Inn, but when I called there, neither of them were in chambers.

As I was going away, he would be led into the passage to be certain that I was out of the house; and Miss S------ told me that a few days before, he crawled upon his knees and hands up stairs, to see if he could discover, any body harboured there, so powerful even at this time, was his passion of suspicion.

The next morning, I called in Lincoln's Inn, and saw Mr. ROBBINS, Mr. MEREDITH being out of town. I told Mr. ROBBINS all the circumstances of my errand: He appointed to meet me at Bowes's; he took a gentleman with him. On our coming, we found there a sister of Bowes's, just arrived in London from Ireland, and who had never seen her brother before. Here also came into our company, Mr. SAMPSON PERRY, who had been attending Bowes in a friendly and medical capacity, for some time previous to this dangerous state.

All being now assembled, as if from sympathy, all were devoted to see if Bowes could be prevailed upon to give any thing to Miss S------. It ought not

to be omitted that Bowes's sister, from the goodness
of her heart, had at her own expence, called in the
CLERGYMAN of the parish. With these powerful
engines; with the particular address of Mr. Sampson
Perry, with the intercession of all around him, with
the begging of the CHILDREN, advancing to the
bedside, one after the other, Bowes at length gave
way, opened his mouth, and consented to Miss S---
having one hundred per annum. This being avowed
to Mr. Perry by Bowes, and legally put down by
Mr. ROBBINS, witnessed by him, his friend, and
myself, we took our leave. I ought to observe,
that there was not a shilling in the house, till Mr.
ROBBINS left a sum, to whose conduct in particular,
I am not now, nor hope ever to be, insensibly forget-
ful. It was a ready display of direct humanity
upon this necessitous occasion.

Bowes survived this transaction not more than
six days. He died on the 16th of January, 1810,
and was buried on the 23rd, in the vault in St.
George's church in the Borough. Two mourning
coaches attended his funeral. Mr. Meredith, (his
executor,) and Bowes's three sons, went in the first,
and the Marshall's relations, Mr. Sampson Perry,
and myself, in the second. No other legacies I
understand are in his will than those to his children
by Miss S-----. His son by the Countess was to
have been his heir.

And here closes the mortal scene of Andrew
Robinson Bowes; whose ruin was finally precipi-
tated from want of moral principle and personal

courage. If he had happened to have been a man
of courage, as well as infamy, he would with his
talent have maintained that which infamy alone
had put into his possession; and he would have
mounted, instead of sunk, as he basely did in the
close of his life: but his mind was treacherous and
inconstant even to itself. 'He was a villain to the
back-bone!! '

That he was not a man of courage is to be seen
in every action of his life; as all his atchievements
were begun and ended without a display of one
single trait of personal heroism. His acts were
violent, and his contrivances always so planned as
to preserve his own person and to immolate every
other man's. His resources were all selfish, mean,
and contemptible. When he seized the person of
the Countess, and carried her into the North, he
denied his concern in it, and kept himself in the
back-ground ; and, when she was in his possession,
he endeavoured to obtain his ends of her by terror,
until he found that even she had a mind possessed
of courage superior to his own. He submitted to
be attacked by a man who knocked him off his
horse, and to have his pistol, without any energetic
effort, wrenched from his hand. He surrendered
it to real courage, on demand, and unarmed.

In every turn of his affairs, his passion indicated
all the sufferings of a coward, without the smallest
show of fortitude. Upon the loss of his first cause
'in the Common Pleas, before Lord Rosslyn, he fell
into a state of deplorable despondence: and now

grown older, when he lost the second before Sir
James Mansfield in the year 1807, he sunk never to
rise again.

Bowes was incapable of making friends, for he
did not wish to know any thing of the quality of
friendship. The friend with whom he formerly
corresponded, had long given him over, and detached himself from him, after suffering in fame
and in fortune. On his last trial in the Court of
Common Pleas, Bowes not being able to attend
about it, and to bustle himself in it, seduced from
the West of England the husband of his own
daughter. He travelled for him into the North for
evidence, and all at his own expence. He was
taught to believe that a very large legacy at least
was intended; or if otherwise, that his wife would be
Bowes's heiress. The hopes of this gentleman were
also disappointed. Bowes considered all females
as natural game, and hunted them down as so many
FERÆ NATURÆ. Under the cloak of friendship he
made instruments of mankind as he called for
them, and in his arts of seduction he refined above
all others.

All those who served him the most essentially
and gratified him the longest, he treated with the
most severity. They were left at length to feel
disgrace from their own mortifying reflections.
The very yearnings of nature were struck dumb
with astonishment at him. Open resentment was
suppressed by shameful remorse, and the injured

withheld their vengeance, and slunk away from him, silent, degraded, and astounded.

He cloathed all his villainies in the dress of virtue; and it is something to be told, that this bad man could not succeed in perpetrating acts of vice, without assuming the appearance of virtue. To sum up his character in a few words, he was cowardly, insidious, hypocritical, tyrannic, mean, violent, selfish, deceitful, jealous, revengeful, inhuman, and savage, without a single countervailing quality.

Let us hope, when he, departed ; that never before nor since, there never was, nor ever will be, taking him for all in all, his parallel.

The great object of every piece of biography is to produce out of it a wholesome and exemplary MORAL. As ROCKS in the ocean are set down in charts, for instruction to mariners to be cautious and careful to avoid them, so may these well authenticated and dangerous LIVES become useful and important to mankind, by the warning they will continue to give to future generations.

FINIS.

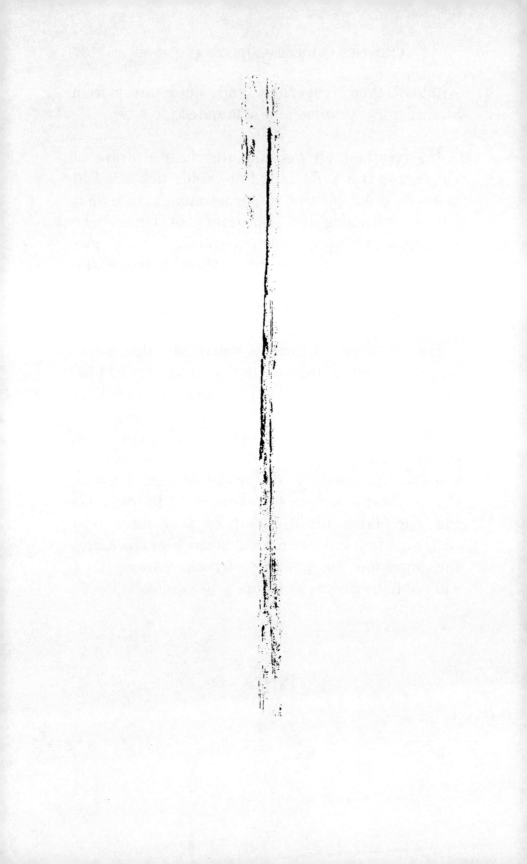

CHIRURGICAL WORKS

JESSÉ FOOT.

1 A Critical Enquiry into the Ancient and Modern Methods, of Curing Diseases in the Urethra and Bladder. Fifth Edition, 2s 6d.

2 Cases of the successful Practice of VESICÆ LOTURA, in the Cure of Diseased Bladders, 4s 6d.

3 A Treatise on Syphilis and Diseases in the Urethra, Bladder, and Kidnies, 4to. 1l 10s.

4 Dialogues between a Pupil of John Hunter and Jessé Foot, 3s.

5 Life of John Hunter, 5s 6d.

6 Observations on the New Opinions of John Hunter, 8s 6d.

7 An Essay on the Bite of a Mad Dog, with a Plan, 2s 6d.

8 A new-discovered Fact in the Action of Syphilis, 6d.

9 Important Researches upon the Existence, Nature, and Communication of Syphilis in Pregnant Women, New-born Infants, and Nurses, 3s 6d.

Sold by T. BECKET and PORTER, Pall Mall, and HIGHLEY, Fleet-Street.

CPSIA information can be obtained at www.ICGtesting.com
Printed in the USA
BVOW02s1126220316

441291BV00027B/362/P